BUDE

THE POSTCARD COLLECTION

Dawn G. Robinson

AMBERLEY

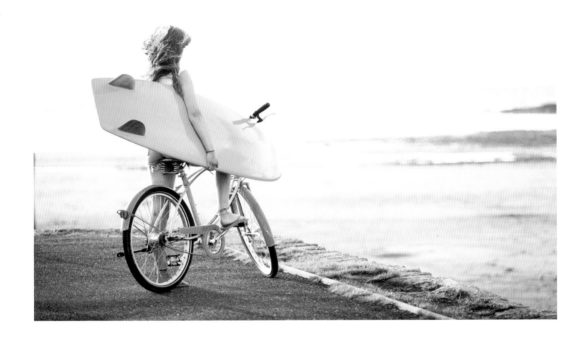

First published 2015

Amberley Publishing
The Hill, Stroud, Gloucestershire, GL5 4EP
www.amberley-books.com

Copyright © Dawn G. Robinson, 2015

The rights of Dawn G. Robinson to be identified as the
Author of this work has been asserted in accordance with
the Copyrights, Designs and Patents Act 1988.

ISBN 978 1 4456 4523 0 (print)
ISBN 978 1 4456 4531 5 (ebook)

British Library Cataloguing in Publication Data.
A catalogue record for this book is available from the
British Library.

Typesetting by Amberley Publishing.
Printed in Great Britain.

ACKNOWLEDGEMENTS

I am indebted, as ever, to local postcard collector and historian, Ray Boyd, without whom this book would not have been possible. Ray has supplied most of the postcards and contributed to some of the text. Other images have been provided by Malcolm Mitchell; again, many thanks are due. Contemporary card images are from Bude Area Tourist Board, so thanks also to Mark from the Tourist Information Centre.

Also, to the late Rennie Bere and Bryan Dudley Stamp, whose detailed book *The Book of Bude and Stratton* (1980) has been a wonderful checking device. It was an absolute pleasure to once meet Bryan, and later to be granted access to his collection of materials, so thanks indeed to his son, Jonathan Stamp.

A mention, also, for the historical image website I share with locals, Ray Boyd and Rob Wilcox, containing many images of Bude, freely accessible to all, though nothing beats having a lovely book in one's hand containing high resolution images like these. The website is www.bude-past-and-present.org.uk. Readers of the site and the Facebook page also helped with a few historical queries. Thank you all. If any mistakes have been made, despite all the cross-checking, then that is down to me.

Finally, to my wonderful daughter, Rosie Walsh, for quite decisively helping me to choose the images, and for noticing things I hadn't spotted.

INTRODUCTION

The welcoming, friendly, family holiday resort of Bude is much loved by locals and visitors alike. It remained off the beaten track and remarkably undeveloped until the coming of the canal in the early 1800s, with neighbouring Stratton far more important.

People had no reason to go to Bude and the roads were difficult. For contrast, we have included a few images from old Stratton, a town adjacent to Bude; the two now share a town council. There are also some images of surrounding villages, such as Poughill and Marhamchurch, to give a taste of the varied but rural flavour of this largely coastal area of North Cornwall.

Before the 1800s, the sea around Bude was considered very treacherous. Building the sea canal, which opened up Bude, creating work and thus encouraging inward migration of population, was a true feat of engineering skill; the canal remains a key feature of the town with its sea lock and, inland, a series of unusual inclined planes, used for the wheeled tub boats to carry sand to farmland. The canal lock gates have taken many a battering from high seas. Even as recently as 2008 one of the gates was wrenched off. With the canal, trade built, as did warehouses and accommodation; the former diminished, but the accommodation was put to improved use. The much later coming of the railway, in 1898, helped to put Bude on the map, this time as a popular Victorian tourist destination.

People, the wealthy and workers alike, saw the therapeutic qualities of sea bathing, becoming desirous of taking to the waters. Visitors came from places like London, or closer, from inland Cornish towns like Launceston. A Bude volunteer archivist mentions catching the local Waterloo milk train at 1 a.m. and arriving at 8 a.m. While this account was as late as 1955, the train links were vital in developing Bude as a tourist town.

As tourism blossomed, postcards became exceptionally important. They were a key way of keeping in touch without too much effort. With cheap postage, they were a good way to show people where you were on holiday. The heyday of the postcard was 1890–1920, but the views available from Bude were rather limited then, as you can see from the collection. However, they remain a wonderful way of seeing how the resort has changed. Fashions in greetings cards also change. Some cards were hand-coloured, in itself a controversial practice, and people often wrote on the front of postcards, something we rarely do today.

By 1926, Bude had a glut of boarding houses, some of which were quite large, to cater for sizeable households and staff from the 'quality' who visited, alongside the five main hotels. Today Bude has even more. It is on the up and even has its own successful Bude Food Festival. Always a genteel family resort, it attracted 'well-to-do' holidaymakers to places like the prestigious Grenville Hotel which, even today, as Adventure International, dominates Bude's skyline.

In this collection of cards, mainly owned by a local lifelong collector, Ray Boyd, we have postcards from Valentine, Frith, Judges (who dated their cards) and other lesser-known manufacturers, whose images can only be dated by content such as clothing. The market for local postcards in Bude was pretty much cornered by the Thorn family. This well-known local

5

photographic family originated from nearby Kilkhampton and Launcells in the sixteenth century, or maybe before according to the book *Views and Likenesses* by Charles Thomas. Some Thorns were also found across the Tamar in adjoining Devon parishes.

The Thorn family members were entrepreneurial. They developed a business empire selling old photographs and postcards of the Bude area, which was still little known at the time. Samuel Thorn, born in 1809, later married, and the couple had many children. First came Harry, who has no baptismal record but was thought to have been born in 1838. He was listed in various records as a 'photographic artist'. Sadly, Harry committed suicide in Bude on 30 October 1876, at thirty-eight years of age; who knows what troubled him. There are many photographs of Bude bearing the name 'Thorn', some being H. Thorn and others S. Thorn. H. Thorn was the aforementioned Harry. S. Thorn was Samuel, baby of the family, born in 1853. A third Thorn joined the family business, this time a sister, called Sarah Pain Thorn, baptised with her unusual name in May 1843. Sarah lived until she was nearly ninety.

Samuel died in 1898, leaving Sarah to carry on and enlarge the family business. Little is known about the history of women in the locality, yet it seems they were also economically productive, so it is wonderful to have her story, for this lady was something of a commercial phenomenon. In 1889, she was advertising her 'Photographic and Stationery Establishment,

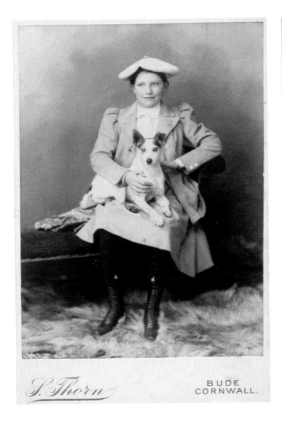

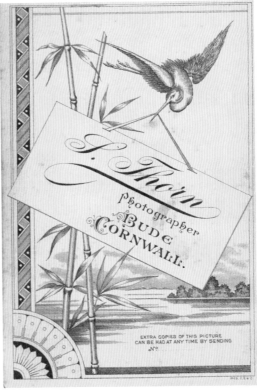

The Crescent' with sea views and portraits. She also had branch outlets at Boscastle and Tintagel, which do not sound too distant but were quite a jaunt in those times. Her advertisement mentioned Thorn's Circulating Library and 'Horses and Carriages Let on Hire'. Quite the businesswoman, and seemingly full of energy, Sarah was still active around 1900, editing a small local paper, *The Bude Gazette and Visitor's Guide,* and using the large family stock of photographs as postcards to sell.

The Thorns were huge in Bude. They knew their area very well indeed, got to places which were still very difficult to reach on foot and had very little competition. They specialised in storms, wrecks and lifeboats. Other local postcard publishers were J. H. Petherick of Bude and Broad of Bude.

Towards the end of the book, it felt right to include some contemporary 2015 postcards, produced by the Bude Area Tourist Board (from where they may be purchased), to illustrate beautiful Bude as it is today and further demonstrate how representations of the area have changed over time.

From old practices of merely showing places and spaces, postcards have moved on to inspiring families to engage in activities, as reflected in these images for the 2015 postcard collection (not all are included here). Now the focus is less on views and more on 'doing', ideally with a great view, too, as photographic technique has developed and as British seaside holidays become less focused on passive visiting and more about engaging.

Enjoy a tour of Bude's past and present through this carefully selected but extensive postcard collection.

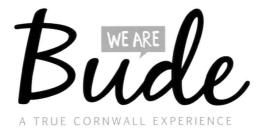

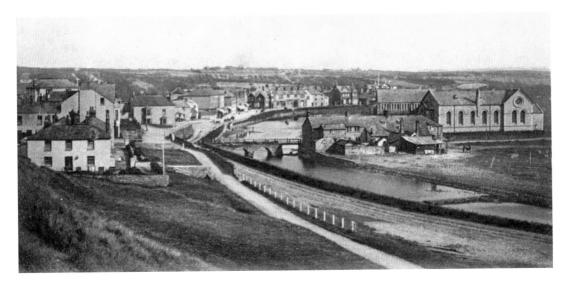

Summerleaze Down

Compare two postcards of the same place. The first is entitled Bude From Compass Point, which does not look feasible, so perhaps some poetic licence was at play. The Compass Point, a former coastguard lookout, is situated on Efford Down, across the river and canal to the Breakwater area. Built of local sandstone by the Acland family, it moved to Efford Down in 1880, which is where it would have stood when this postcard was mailed on 30 August 1904. It looks more like a view from the town end of Summerleaze Down. The very similar image (*below*) was posted on 14 July 1903. Curiously, people used to scribble notes on the front of the cards. The sender, Nell, complains of rather dull weather. This card is more accurately entitled The Strand and River, Bude. It was known by locals as the 'River', but now tends to be called the River Neet, or by some, the Strat. The Strat feeds from the north and the Neet from the south – the Neet being a tributary of the Strat, both forming the main Bude river, which is liable to dramatic flooding at times, usually around once every ten years.

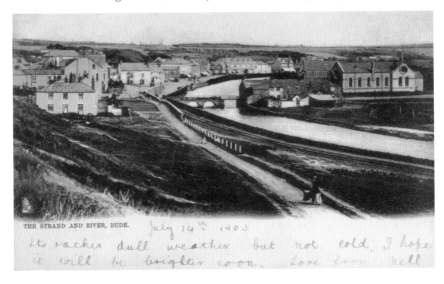

THE STRAND AND RIVER, BUDE. *July 14th 1903*

Its rather dull weather but not cold, I hope it will be brighter soon. Love from nell

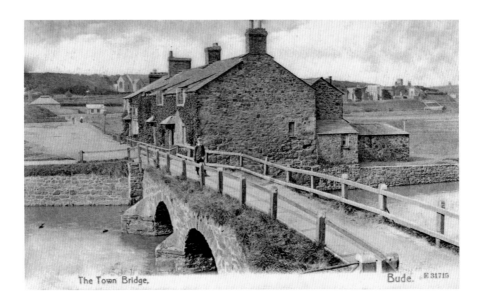

The Town Bridge, Bude. E31715

Nanny Moore's Bridge

Everyone loves the landmark that is Nanny Moore's Bridge, originally known as the Town Bridge. The Grade II listed bridge is a packhorse and cart bridge across the River Neet, dating from the eighteenth century or even earlier. It is a stone rubble three-span bridge with segmental arches, which now only carries pedestrians. Nanny Moore was a real person who lived in one of Levens Cottages next to the bridge. She was a 'dipper' or bathing machine attendant for those women wishing to enter the sea. From 1894, check out the view of a rather full river and Old Bridge from the other side, the Strand direction, probably near what would now be the Bencoolen Bridge. You can see the Bude Hotel, believed to have opened in 1780, where the TSB bank is now situated at the Triangle. You travel this way to enter Bude, and this area of the town was always well served by coaches leaving the Bude Hotel site for Okehampton and other towns.

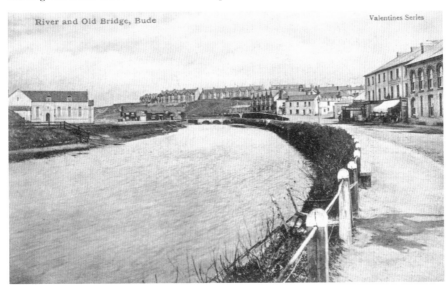

River and Old Bridge, Bude   Valentines Series

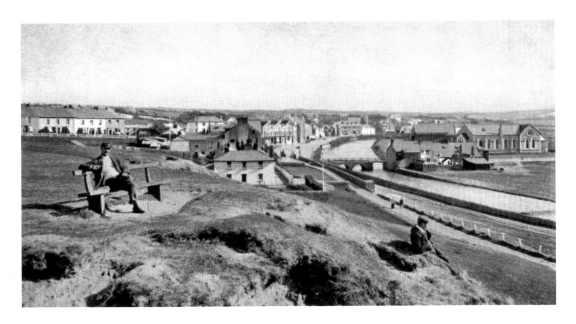

Summerleaze Down and Nanny Moore's Bridge

The coloured card is taken from Summerleaze Down (spelling here is Summerlease). Summerleaze Down, was, according to local historians Bere and Dudley Stamp, sold to Bude & Stratton Unitary District Council by Col G. Thynne, who had previously sold other Down land for golf course use. This position on the Down provides an excellent view over the Strand end of Bude. Although it is the same area, the close up view of Nanny Moore's Bridge shows what was then a track, but is now the roadway for cars to Summerleaze car park. The bridge, formerly known as Bude Bridge, is now only a footbridge. A 'passe' over the river at Efford Hill is mentioned in a contemporary account of the Battle of Stamford Hill in 1643, which may refer to this one. The area to the right of the picture could originally be lifted to allow boats to pass through. The postcards date from around 1900 to 1905.

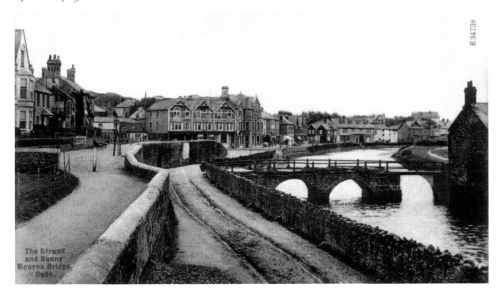

The Strand and Nanny Moores Bridge, Bude.

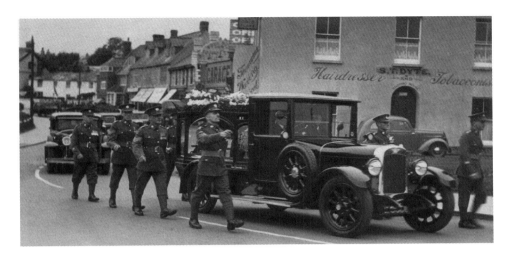

Bude Funeral

Bude has numerous military links, but no one seems to know whose funeral this is, which is a mystery. According to local postcard collector Ray Boyd, the car in the background looks like a Vauxhall 10 Series, which first appeared in 1937, so the image was probably taken sometime in the 1940s. Bude has something of a military history despite escaping the worst ravages of war, apart from obvious human loss of those who went away to fight. Before the First World War, Bude had gently expanded and horses were gathered and supplied for the war effort, *War Horse* style. By 1938, the Ministry of Defence purchased Cleave Farm, above Coombe Valley as an anti-aircraft practice range. Military training was undertaken here and a convalescent home for soldiers nursed many back to health. Clifton College was also evacuated to Bude to escape air raids on Bristol in 1941. In 1943, the Americans arrived, training on Maer Cliff and at nearby Sandymouth. Still in the Strand area of town, Nanny Moore's Bridge in the 1880s had a rather dangerous drop to the river with no wall or fencing, and a view out beyond to the ships and the harbour. Originally, the bridge was partly cantilevered to allow passage of boats. Everyone knows the bridge was renamed after the 'dipper' who lived nearby, but the question is why? Perhaps she was something of a character. What did she do to have a bridge named after her?

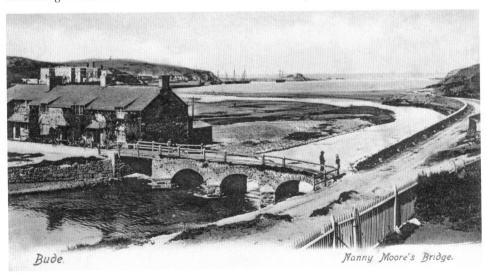

Bude.   Nanny Moore's Bridge.

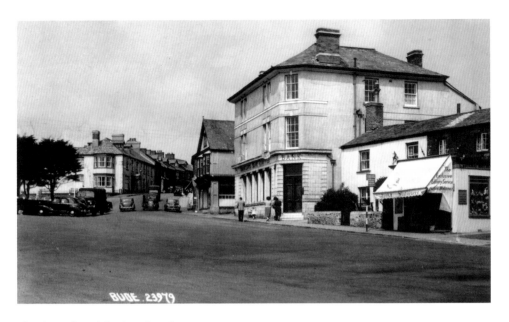

The Strand and Station Road

In the 1950s, Bude had a busy railway station, and the Strand would be the entry into the town if using transport from the station or walking, as the station was situated where the Rugby Club now is. On these cards, the Strand looks quiet, with a few cars, a rather prominent Barclays bank building (still there) and a bookshop/stationers. The Strand is still very much the gateway into Bude; it has had mixed fortunes and looks rather different now to how it did back in 1905 and indeed 1955, with a few developments taking place; it is a place of constant change and improvement. The second view is from Station Road and you can see the horse and donkey carts. The road looked in a fairly serious state of disrepair, befitting a donkey track. The direction of the traffic is curious, for the carts seem to be driving on the right. You can see that everyone captured in the image is wearing a hat.

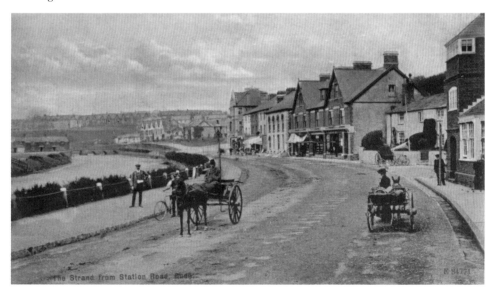

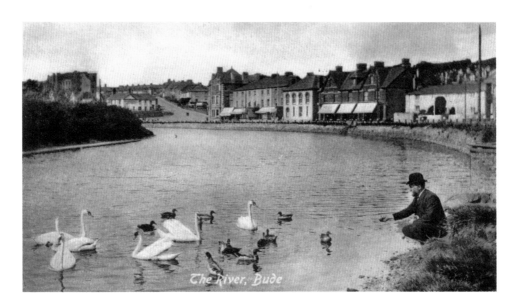

The River, Bude

The Neet and the Strand

In 1911, the Neet was still called 'The River' and the pastoral image of a businessman in a bowler hat feeding the ducks is an interesting one, as most cards show people at leisure rather than booted and suited; presumably he is taking a break from work. The ducks and swans now tend to congregate more on the Bude Canal (probably as people use the canal wharf and therefore food is more readily available) than the river, where one occasionally sees a heron and recently, some brightly coloured kingfishers. The 1905 postcard of the Strand shows some of the shops available and the Carriers Inn, which has a horse and cart or carriage outside. The Carriers, the oldest inn in town, has now been revamped and is currently painted pale blue. The road off to the right of the Bude Hotel, one of Bude's first hotels, is Belle Vue and the main thoroughfare in the town was described by Canon Maskell in 1863 as a 'moderately sloping hill'.

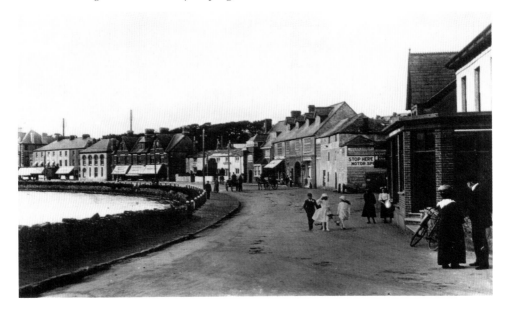

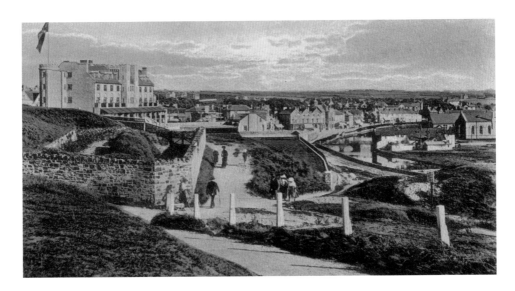

The Downs

The thoroughfare from the river up to the Downs, or in this case, for some, the Grenville Hotel, is a pleasant one. This hand-coloured view (by someone especially enthusiastic about the grassed areas) gives a vision of the town as it developed. Public rights on the Downs were once squabbled over. The Thynne family wished to build a 150-room hotel on the Downs called The Granville, near what is now the cricket ground. The commoners were understandably up in arms at this infringement of their rights to graze donkeys. They won the fight and the hotel idea was abandoned. By 1922, there were cars on the streets of Bude. You can see an automobile in this picture parked outside the Strand Garage, which Southern National took over in the 1930s. The card also shows Cook's Stores, which was a grocery. Each store has an awning onto the street front, which added a certain allure to the area. The Strand was a busy thoroughfare but seems to have declined in importance as Belle Vue developed. The Strand was originally the site of warehouses (one where the Strand Hotel stands and one where the Strand Shopping Arcade, also known as Julia's Place, lies) but Belle Vue was still not complete by 1846.

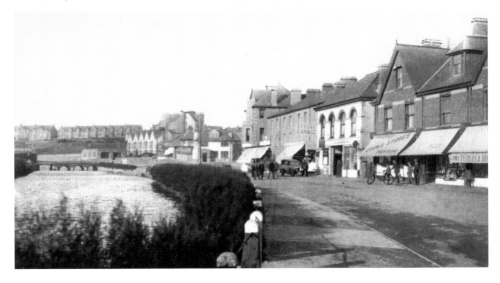

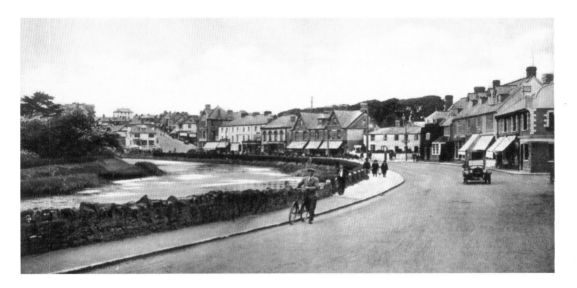

The Strand

By 1928, the country was moving towards the Depression, and automobile sales began to drop. There remains an occasional car around in the image on this first card, but people were largely walking or cycling, perhaps conscious of costs. Not sure why the gentleman is wheeling his bike on one of the few flat bits of land; maybe he was just enjoying the view. Compare with a much more modern view of the Strand from the 1950s in the Francis Frith card. By now we have people awaiting buses, and many more cars on the streets. The Strand at this time was quite a busy little spot – a terminus for buses to the town. I wonder what changed it into the rather quiet shopping area is it today; presumably more commercial in-town development along Belle Vue, Queen Street and Lansdown Street, which shifted the focus. The Globe Hotel is looking much more dominant than it does today, too. Originally on the site was The Jolly Sailor, a little inn which sold ale and spirits to the sailors and carters who collected sand to transport along the canal.

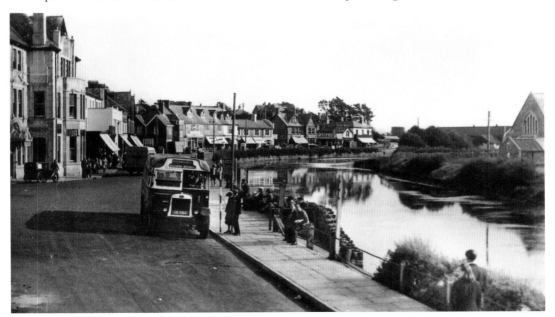

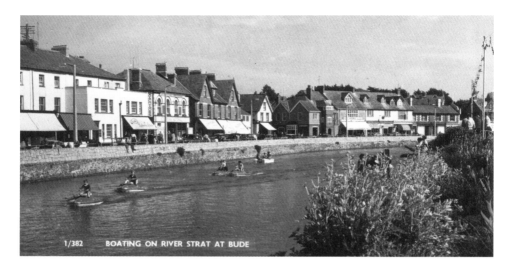

1/382 BOATING ON RIVER STRAT AT BUDE

River Strat and Recreation Grounds

By 1961, the river became known as the River Strat, and people went boating on it. The children looked to be having great fun on what look like forerunners of the jet ski. Now, all boating seems to take place on Bude Canal rather than the river. In the storms of 2014, the river received national news coverage when adrenaline-fuelled local surfers river-surfed in extreme conditions. It was amazing to watch. Looking at the shops, we begin to see that coach tours are advertised as a holiday option. There is also a Southern National shop or office. While most of Cornwall was served by Western National buses, Bude, due to its LSWR/Southern Railway connections, had a Southern National service. At last some photographic colour began to appear on the postcards in 1962, though the colours look rather overly vibrant here. Not much else had changed other than cars parked, perhaps a sign of parking needs to come. The rather laissez-faire car parking arrangement has long gone. It is a good shot of the gentlemen bowling at the recreation ground, readily viewed across the river, neatly tucked away behind the tennis courts. The recreation grounds opened in 1924 on reclaimed land between the castle and Nanny Moore's Bridge.

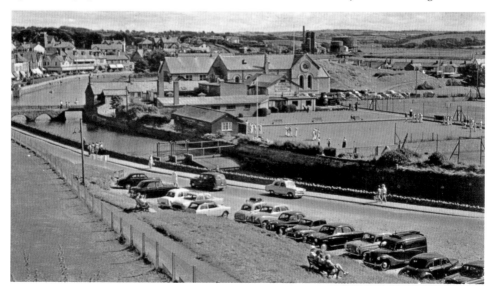

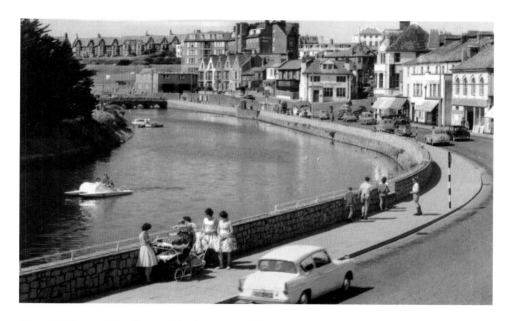

From the Turn of the Twentieth Century to the Swinging Sixties

Now we really have reached the swinging 1960s (*above*) with this postcard dating from 1963. Pedal boats on the river, brightly coloured cars (in the forefront, a Ford Anglia) and the ladies wearing flattering frocks, while the men don their shorts, is a snapshot of the time. How the fashions change, as reflected in this card. Even some of the buildings are brightly painted. Lloyds Bank was by then in situ at the bottom of Belle Vue/Triangle area, and the Grenville Hotel was still a major presence. The river may have been that blue; it certainly doesn't look it now, but it is still an attractive area in summer. Below is a lovely image of the Carrier's Inn, Bude, from the early 1900s. Even then, it was boasting its considerable history, being over 200 years old. The Carriers, an old manor farmhouse, is the oldest building in the Strand, dating back to the seventeenth century. The proprietress at this time was Miss A. Cobbledick. Outside is a stagecoach. There are an amazing fourteen people on top of the coach, preparing for what must have been a hellish journey. The coach driver, Frank Cobbledick, stands behind the horses.

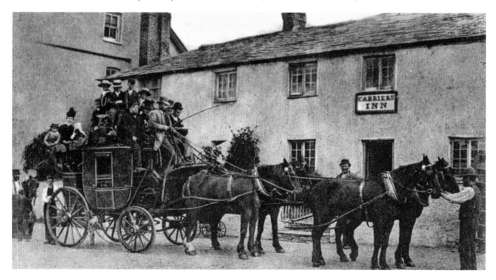

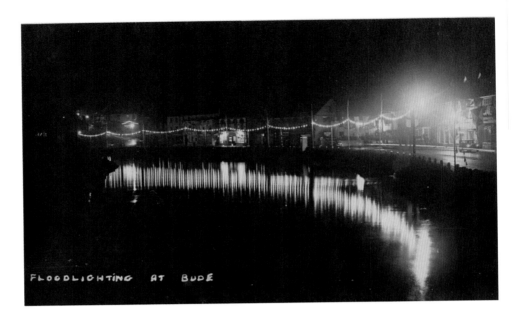

FLOODLIGHTING AT BUDE

Leven Cottages

The Coronation of King George VI took place in 1937, after the abdication of his brother, Edward VIII, over his marriage to divorcee Wallace Simpson. Having lights along the Strand is not a new idea, but they were definitely in situ in 1937, as they are today, making the area quite well lit at night. The quality of this postcard is not great but the floodlighting reflected in the river creates quite a glow. Leven Cottages, near Nanny Moore's Bridge, were ivy clad in the early 1900s. Leven is linked with Efford Mill and the grinding of flour. The oldest cottage in Bude, close to the bridge, has a granite block in the wall inscribed as 'AJA 1589', which is the uniting of Anne and John Arundel, an old Bude family. For over 400 years, Bude was owned by two families and their kin, the Arundels and Aclands on one side of the river and the Grenvilles and Thynnes on the other; their lasting influence may be seen in the buildings and development of the town.

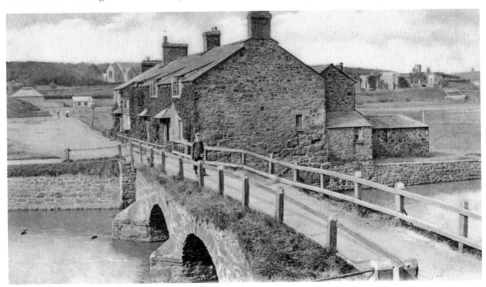

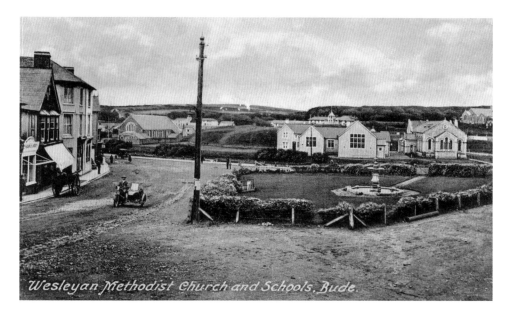

Wesleyan Methodist Church and Schools, Bude.

The Triangle

The Triangle here offers a view to the Wesleyan Methodist church and schools as they were in 1920. On this coloured postcard, a motorbike and sidecar wend their way up Lansdown Road, while a pony and cart waited outside Wonnacott's Dairy. They delivered milk daily from the churn. There were no trees growing in the Triangle in 1920, as there are now, but, at the left-hand edge is the block of granite that formed the outlet for the main town water supply before the mains was connected; this was used later as a wishing well. The telegraph wires were painted out of the original photo for the final postcard. The Strand and Nanny Moore's Bridge, 1906, is also a Frith image. This image is much improved by the costumes of the people at the forefront. The clothing is very much of its time, especially the children's hats. Yet, the rest of the place appears deserted. How did Frith manage it? Now this is quite a busy pathway, rarely seen like this.

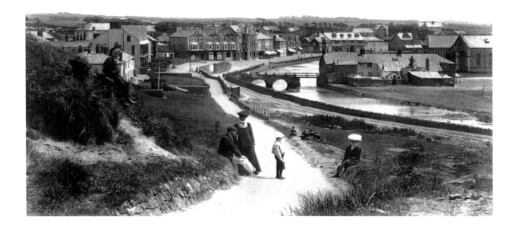

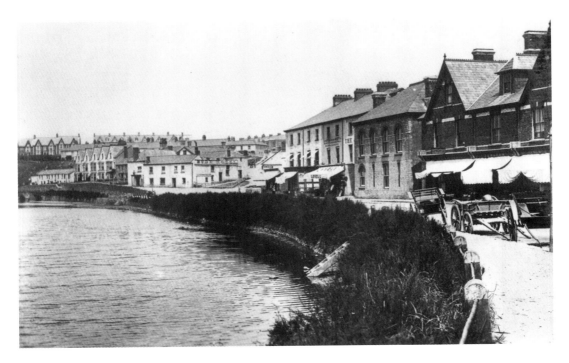

The Strand, Home of Bude Fair
A lovely 1895 image of the Strand, with carts and shops, including Densham's, Lovell's, the Globe Inn run by Nanny Wilson and the slightly dilapidated looking frontage of the Bude Hotel. Note the little ladder down to the river, presumably there for maintenance or boating purposes. The Strand was also home to the Bude fair, seen below in 1911.

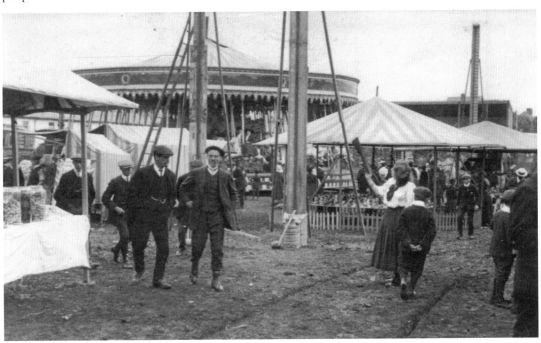

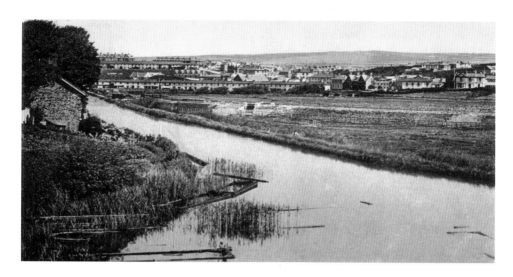

Bude from the Canal

Here, we see Bude from the canal around 1900. Bude local Ray Boyd explains, 'This card is looking from the bulge in the canal (which marks an old quarry) towards the town, about 1890. Baulks of timber float in the canal next to the Bude Haven Saw Mill (later the Steam Laundry), ready for cutting into planks for use in the adjacent Stapleton's boat yard. What is now the marshes was a water meadow, stretching unbroken up to the Crescent. The area near the canal was obviously built up considerably when the railway was built a few years later. On the skyline, Summerleaze Crescent is still under construction, with scaffolding around one block and empty window frames.' The postcard below shows several ships waiting to lock out in the canal and several more in the harbor – a reminder of Bude's shipping history. The image shows (the two nearest the locks) the *Infanta* (a schooner), *Elizabeth* (a ketch, with two masts) and, to the right, *Mirre* (a smack, a traditional fishing boat). You can also see the rail line to the beach and several tub boats. Bude Canal was not even considered a possibility until 1774 when the plan was put forward to connect the haven to the Tamar.

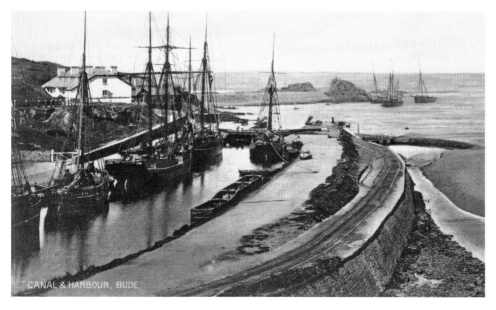

CANAL & HARBOUR, BUDE.

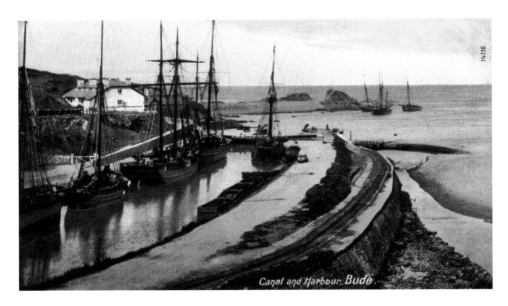

Canal and Harbour, Bude.

Bude Haven

This is the same image as on the previous page but this time in colour, bringing it to life, making it look really quite different, with the sky reflected in the water. Bude Haven was a port long before the canal was contemplated. Bude had a master of the port as early as 1535, and near Nanny Moore's Bridge was an old quay. By 1774, however, although the canal was considered, it was found to be economically unattractive. When you walk by the canal now, this is not a sight you will see, but how wonderful it must have looked to see these sizeable ships. This tinted postcard from 1911 (*below*) shows two ketches waiting to lock out; one is the *Bristol Packet,* built at Newport in 1857, the other the *Susanna,* built at Appledore in 1860. In the background to the left is the old rocket house on Breakwater Road, which stored lifesaving rocket launch equipment for the breeches buoy rope, so essential for sailing ships on this treacherous coast.

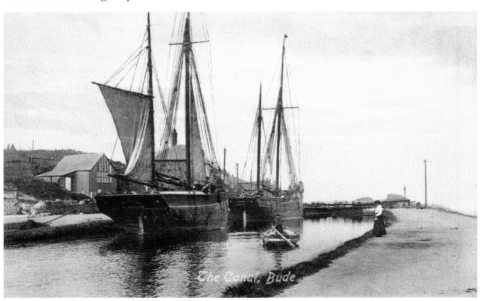

The Canal, Bude

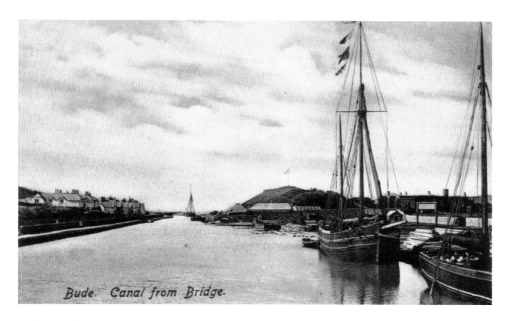

Bude. Canal from Bridge.

Bude Canal

This sepia postcard is Bude Canal from the bridge near the Falcon, and dates from around 1890. The ship may be the ketch, *Alford,* owned by John Banbury of Bude with J. B. Cook as master; if it was, she was later lost in a gale on the passage to Hamburg in 1922. Many of the old sea captains lived handily in the now highly desirable Breakwater Road and the canal labourers tended towards Falcon Cottages. Although this busy 1898 card below is entitled 'Sports in Bude', it is actually an image of Lifeboat Day (which, to be fair, usually incorporates some canal-based sport), with the crowds lining the canal lower basin and harbour area, as they still do today. The RNLI has always been treasured and valued in Bude, where the RNLI men are local heroes. Lifeboat Day takes place annually in late August in the town, and is one of the largest fundraising events. Here, the Falcon Bridge still has the old construction; the railway bridge over the river is built but it appears that the railway line has not yet reached the wharf, according to local expert Ray Boyd.

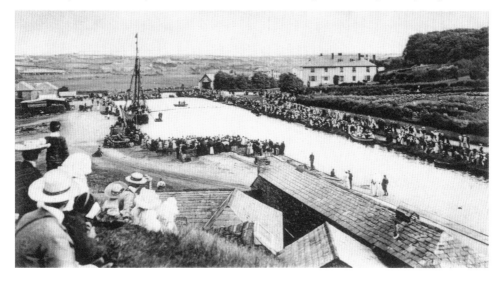

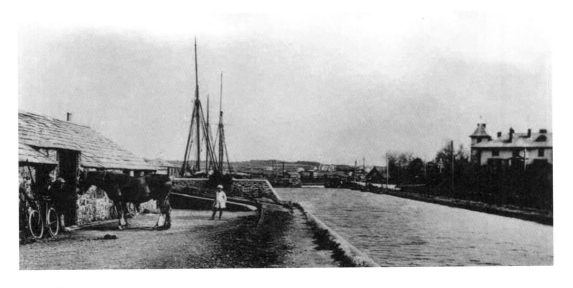

The Old Forge

The old forge is shown here in the 1920s in this Raphael Tuck postcard. The forge and other buildings have been revamped by the Bude & Stratton Town Council and now house predominantly artisan and craft shops shops alongside the canal, but the area has been conserved so does not look that different. The forge originally made and mended parts for tub boats, but later was used mainly for horseshoes, and still later for ornamental items. A side view of the Falcon Hotel is here, tucked away to the right, across the canal. Boats for hire include the veteran motorboat, Verbena, in this card from the 1920s. The Verbena saw many years of service. What is interesting is that the hire pitch is on the Breakwater side of the canal, whereas now all the boat hire is across on the other side of the canal, with this side largely used by fishing enthusiasts. Now most of the boats are rowing boats or pedalos.

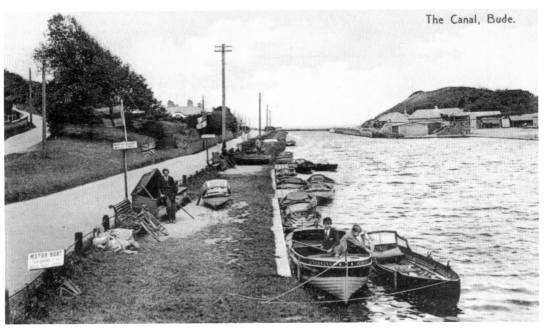

The Canal, Bude.

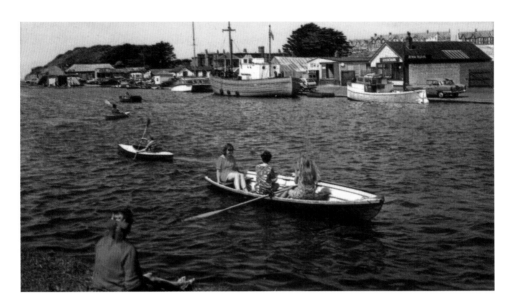

From the Canal Path

Looking a tad choppy, a colour shot of the canal from the over-enhanced and colour-clashing 1970s, or is it actually the late 1960s? Loving the minidress, the psychedelic prints of the people in the boat and the chiffon hair tie. Does that say Devon Tea Room, too, in the background to the right? Not sure that would go down too well in Bude these days which, while relatively close to the Devon border, remains steadfastly and proudly Cornish. The town celebrates St Piran's Day (the Cornish National Day) on 5 March with a parade along the coastal path and back along the Downs to Crooklets Beach/Bude Surf Life-Saving Club, led by locals to the tune of a Cornish piper. An idyllic scene, not that different to today, is this one of families boating on the canal, though the bridge by the Falcon is somewhat prettier here than it is now. This hand-tinted card dates from the early 1900s, when watercolours and stencils were used, creating a sense of tranquillity still apparent today along the canal path.

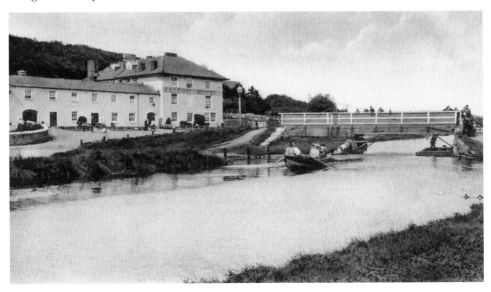

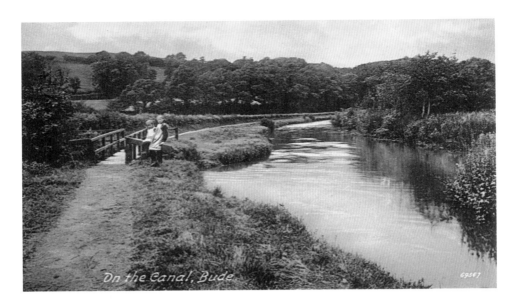

Helebridge

This is a Francis Frith card, showing a tranquil scene on the canal around the hamlet of Helebridge, an area that is prone to river flooding. Helebridge was considered wide enough to take barges of sand and from there the canal went to Red Post, where it branched, one arm towards Holsworthy in Devon and one towards Alfardisworthy, near Kilkhampton (Tamar Lake area). The first inclined plane, a historic feature for which Bude Canal is noted and noteworthy, was from Helebridge to Marhamchurch, powered by waterwheel. The 1920s image shows people again engaged in the sedate art of rowing on the Bude Canal. This is a little away from the town heading towards the weir. It is easy to spend an hour or two rowing on the canal or walking the towpath. Bude Canal and Marsh area is important for engineering history and forms a natural habitat for wildlife. The gentle path is 2.5 miles from Bude to Helebridge. The marsh area is close to the Tourist Information Centre, which is a great place to find out more about the town.

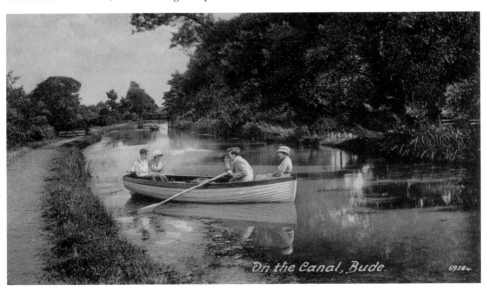

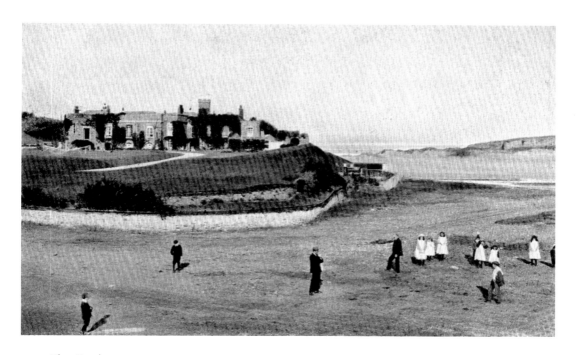

The Castle

The castle is shown here in the 1900s. Rather poor colouring here for the above image of the castle, which was built on a concrete base on shifting sands and home to the Bude inventor (some would say genius) and polymath, Sir Goldsworthy Gurney. You can see the tennis courts in the grounds. The castle is rather more enveloped by other buildings now, but houses a fine, free heritage centre, art exhibitions, a café, and ice cream parlour, so is rightly popular with visitors. A variety of events are held on the castle green throughout the year, including Heritage Day and Lifeboat Day events.

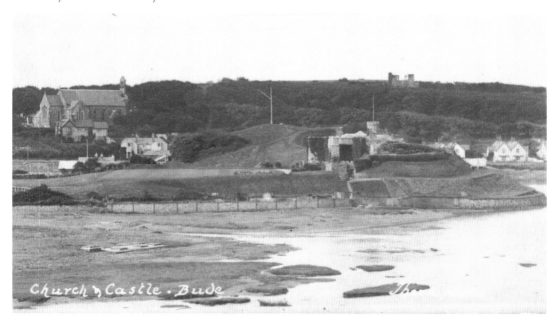

Church & Castle . Bude

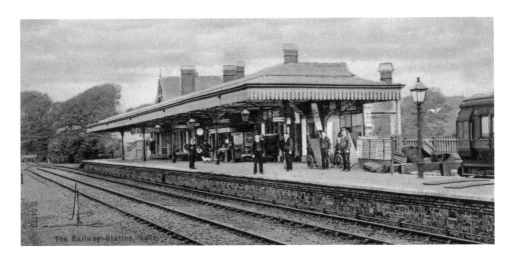

The Railway Station, Bude

Bude Station

Bude station had a long platform for express trains from Waterloo, and a shorter one for local branch trains. They call it progress, but Bude no longer has a station or a direct rail link to London; indeed, there is no rail link to anywhere, though some people are striving to have the troubled Dawlish line (which is coastal and was devastated by winter storms in 2014) rerouted inland through Tavistock and Okehampton, with bus links to Bude. The Beeching axe fell on Bude in 1966, when Bude lost the vital link that was its railway and there were fears that its popularity would wane; luckily, cars still bring visitors to the town. During the Golden Age of Railways, Britain's most powerful passenger engine, with its gold lettering, left Waterloo for Devon and North Cornwall. This was the famous Atlantic Coast Express, which was introduced in 1926. The train would leave Waterloo at 11 a.m. each morning with a through coach to Bude, arriving some 5.5 hours later. Now reaching London involves a drive or bus journey from Bude to Exeter and takes much, much longer. The North Cornwall & Bude Express first ran in 1907. The train split at various points to head off to Devon and Cornwall. The Bude section split from the Padstow section at Halwill Junction. I suspect it was a little confusing for passengers.

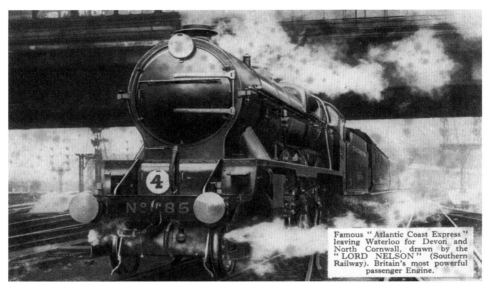

Famous "Atlantic Coast Express" leaving Waterloo for Devon and North Cornwall, drawn by the "LORD NELSON" (Southern Railway). Britain's most powerful passenger Engine.

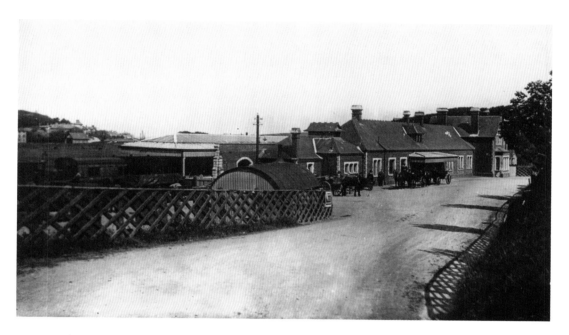

The Station

The above image shows the approach to the London & South Western Railway station, at Bude, around 1910. In this image, horses and carriages await for the onward journey into town and to the hotels. The arrival of the railway meant red bricks were also brought in to build the Thynne family's part of Bude – Summerleaze Crescent, Morwenna Terrace, Burn View and Queen Street. Below is the insignia of the West Country class No. 21C106 BUDE with its initial Cornwall County badge.

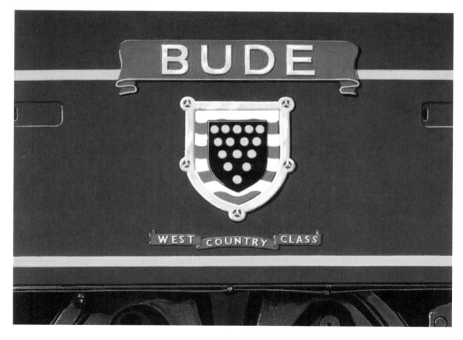

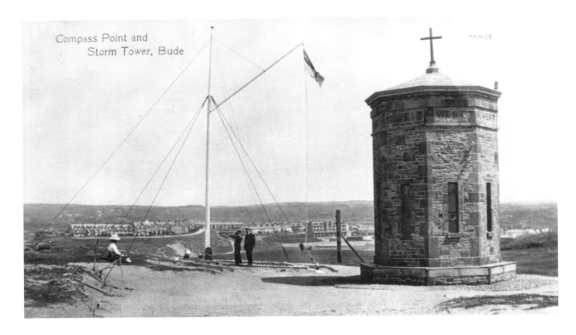

Compass Point and
Storm Tower, Bude

The Storm Tower

The Storm Tower above Compass Point was provided by Thomas Acland, and is a prominent feature of the Bude landscape. Built of local sandstone, with points of the compass carved into its octagonal sides, it is based on the Temple of the Winds at Athens. Locals know it as the Pepper Pot, for fairly obvious reasons. Overlooking Summerleaze, it offers fantastic views along the rugged coastline. Also here we have a rather murky looking panoramic image which does little to make Bude took attractive, demonstrating that early postcard colouring techniques were not always terribly successful. It dates from the early 1900s. Marine Terrace is still standing and Summerleaze looks very underdeveloped on this one. The street at the back, centre right, is King Street, which was then on the outskirts of the town.

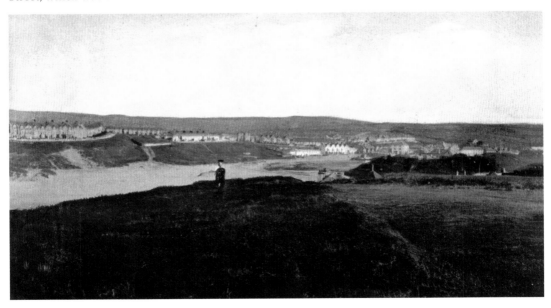

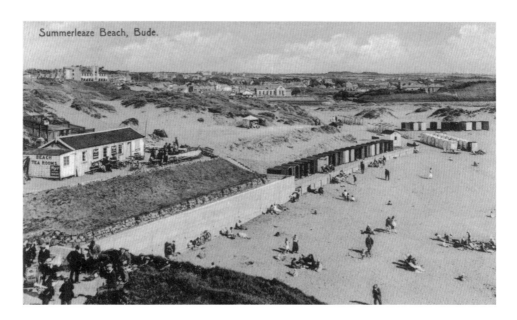

Summerleaze Beach, Bude.

Strolling Spots

Two popular strolling spots. The first shows a band playing on the patch of land above Summerleaze, then known as Mentone Terrace. Originally, according to local postcard collector, Ray Boyd, it was Mentone Quarry, from where a lot of the stone used to build Summerleaze Crescent was obtained (other quarries supplying stone for development were at Stonewall and Flexbury). There was a Mentone Hotel on Breakwater Road. In the centre of the picture is the Beach Tea Rooms, the second of Bude's beach cafés, which followed the Coronation Tea Rooms and was itself replaced by a later beach café in 1929. At the top left, Westcliff House had not yet been converted into the square building of the Westcliff Hotel. Until recently there was a small fish pond built into the cliff here, dedicated to one of Bude's former doctors. Alongside this, we have a rather pleasing card from around 1910, with a delightful young lady walking along the path, wearing contemporary dress. Efford Down remains a popular route to the coastal path and Compass Point, above other inlets close to Bude, due to the spectacular cliff scenery.

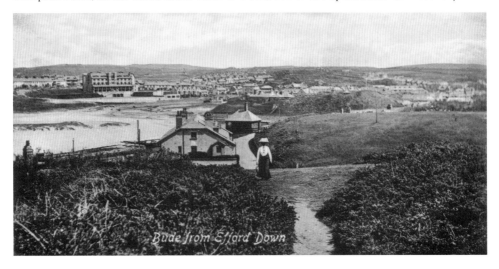

Bude from Efford Down

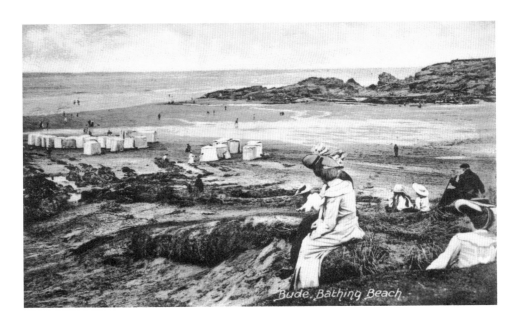

Sea Bathing

Crooklets was the ladies' bathing beach in the days of segregated bathing, complete here with changing tents. Sea bathing really took off once the working classes were able to take holidays and get to the coast; protocols relating to beach attire were still kept in place. Trying to walk the Crooklets rocks in these outfits, complete with large hats, must have been an onerous task. No wonder many ladies sat above the beach and simply drank in the view. No danger of becoming sunburned, anyway! Crooklets was also known as Maer Bathing Beach, as Maer cliff looms above it in Northcott direction. Summerleaze was the male bathing beach. We assume that segregation was all about protecting modesty, but maybe enjoyment also came into it, giving the ladies and gentlemen a well-earned break from each other. Bathing machines were also used to preserve modesty for women especially, but also men, who wished to behave in a proper manner, certainly until the 1860s, when naked male bathing was banned.

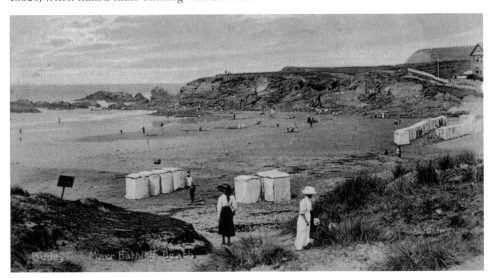

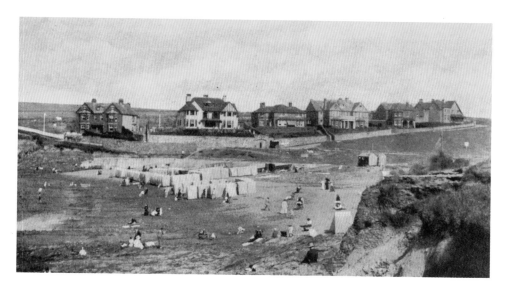

Crooklets

Here, it is called Maer Lake bathing beach, but it remains the ladies' bathing beach at Crooklets. Maer seemed to be dropped as a term in the late 1930s, for some inexplicable reason. Maer Lake itself is a damp hollow in a field (more of a pond) not near to the beach, partly surrounded by housing and liable to flooding after heavy rain. It attracts water-loving birds, such as white-fronted geese and shovelers, but is definitely not for swimming in. This coloured image below dates from the early 1900s when Crooklets is, again, called Maer Lake. The beach was shared by men and women, but no one here is in bathing attire. The history of postcards suggests many were coloured by hand, a process that started in France and Belgium and occurred in an assembly line fashion, with one woman on the line being responsible for a particular colour. Wetting the brush by mouth apparently led to sickness. I'm not sure if the Bude cards were produced in this way, but I cannot think of another method; it was a fairly unhealthy job, and certainly painstaking, probably for scant reward.

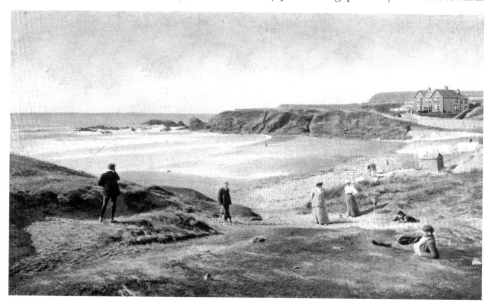

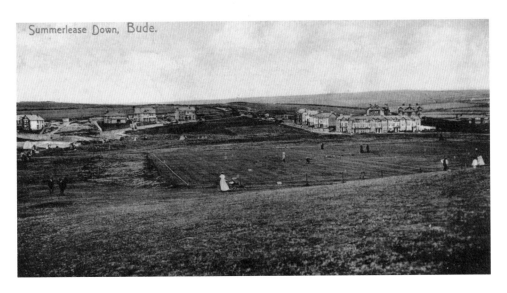

Summerlease Down, Bude.

Summerleaze Down and Maer Beach

Another oddly coloured card of Summerlease Down – or Summerleaze as is it known these days – another one of those peculiar spellings that changed over time. Summerleaze suggests livestock were on the Down in the past, although we already know about the commoners' donkeys. If Bude really was this colour, sunglasses would be a year-round requirement. Another 1900s postcard that makes Bude appear as if covered in moss. It is an interesting place to play tennis, as the area can get quite windy with gusts coming in from the sea, but it demonstrates one of the many uses the Down has been put to over the years. It is now a popular dog-walking spot. Alongside this, we have another postcard of Maer Beach; oddly, there are not many of Middle Beach, which perhaps was as underused then as it often is now. I'm not sure what the structures are, presumably the frames for the beach huts for the ladies to change in privacy. Following the First World War, it became more acceptable to see both sexes wearing bathing costumes; however, changing in public was still frowned upon, a leftover from the days of the cumbersome old bathing machines. Beach huts were provided for changing to avoid fines.

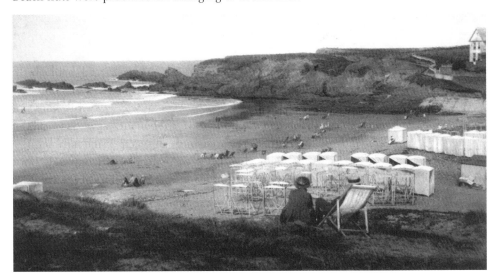

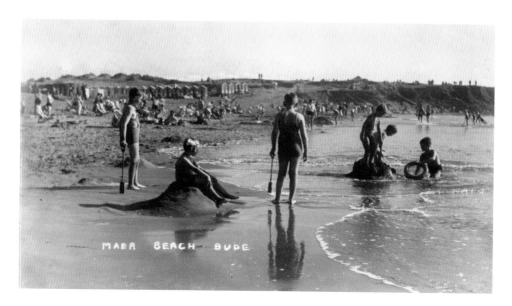

Crooklets

This is said to be Crooklets (Maer Beach) in the 1920s, which looks much livelier than previous pictures, as it is by now attracting families and children for a proper family 'bucket and spade-style' seaside holiday, of the kind that still remains popular in the resort today. The beach huts remain a feature, but car parking, and two very good beach cafés, have also developed in recent years, along with nearby hotels and restaurants, making the Crooklets area much smarter than previously. The image below shows a rather uniform collection of beach huts at Crooklets in the 1930s, which has a holiday camp feel to it (holiday camps were resisted in Bude). However, they do look rather well maintained, which is a big improvement on more modern times, as some have been in a dilapidated state for years, not helped by storms in early 2014. During the storms, some of the Crooklets beach huts were destroyed, mainly the ones close to the Bude Surf Life-Saving Club. Beach huts are now fashionable once again as people develop an interest in vintage fashions.

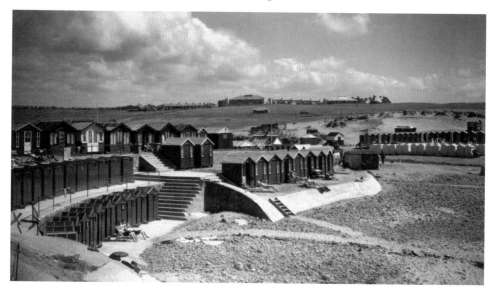

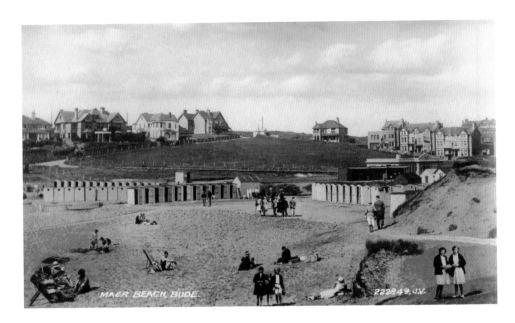

Crooklets

This sepia view of Crooklets is a very strange one. It looks as if the people are somehow stuck on as an afterthought, especially the ones close to the front. As my twenty-first-century daughter exclaimed, 'they look like they have been Photoshopped'. Yet, they are obviously not, as the shadows presumably indicate, and as Photoshop did not exist. Maybe there was a special technique; certainly things did seem to be 'airbrushed' out of images, so may be people could also be added in. The postcard dates from 1933. By the 1950s, we had the heyday of the quintessential British family beach holiday, the image taken during the so-called Golden Age of family, when the annual holiday was a big event and generally taken in England. Quite funny to see that beach attire had not yet changed for the average British man – jacket, pipe and trousers! Perhaps it was a bit chilly that day.

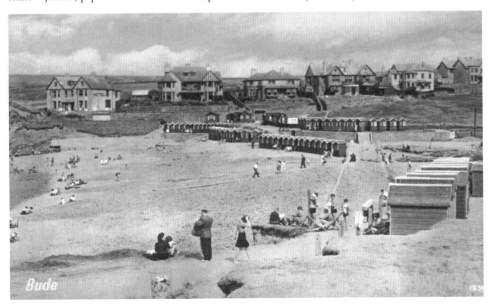

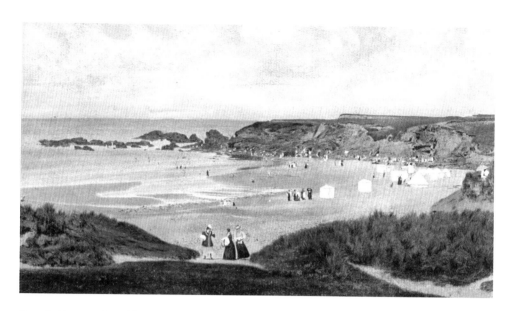

Beach Huts at Crooklets

Image of Crooklets ladies at Maer Beach again. The sexes were carefully segregated, with the men, at this point, mainly sited at Tommy's Pit down at the breakwater. Another hand-tinted one, which does not look terribly natural. It is quite a walk from Tommy's Pit to Maer Beach, so one can only imagine the meeting up arrangements after bathing had finished (no mobile phone communication then). Bathing machines, meanwhile, appeared in 1846, though the term 'resort' had been used for Bude before then. In 1836, it was described as 'The Fashionable Water Place of the West'. Crooklets is also featured here, with lovely bright beach huts dating from the 1970s, before the new beach café was built. These actually look quite cheery, though the heyday of the beach huts was probably in the 1950s. It was a place to get changed with decorum, and they certainly made the area look bright, cared for, and beautiful. However, current plans to build brightly coloured coastal homes near here are attracting some local concern.

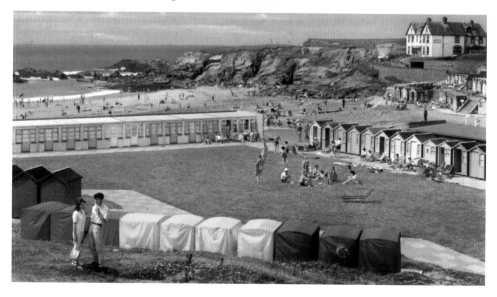

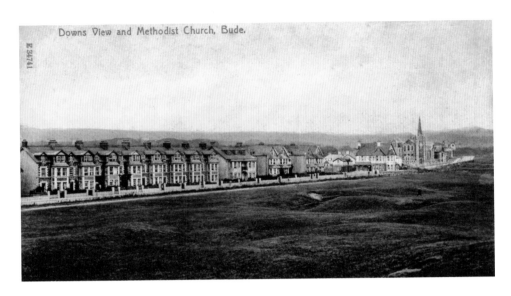

Downs View and Summerleaze Iron Bridge

Another hand-tinted card, with a large expanse of grass, this time of Downs View, dating from the early 1900s. The Methodist church is seen in the distance to the right, now in the area called Flexbury. This slightly eccentric and grandiose-looking church building is Grade II listed, and was built by local builder John Pethick. The church opened in 1905, becoming a United Methodist church, when the Free Methodists and the Bible Christians amalgamated. The church closed in 2008, due to structural problems, but retains its strong visual impact. Moving over to Summerleaze, the card below comes from 1968. Local postcard collector, Ray Boyd writes, 'Originally built to carry the wagons – which traversed an extensive system of rails, much of which now lies beneath Summerleaze Beach – bringing sand to the waiting tub boats on the canal, this is Iron Bridge in 1968. Seen here are an enthusiastic group of people carrying out one of the favourite summer occupations – crabbing! Nothing could beat a few hours, on an incoming tide, watching lines baited with fish heads from Mike Scown or Hedley Troke at Macfisheries and waiting for a hungry crab which, if caught, was carefully stored in a bucket until the end of the day, and then tipped back for next time.'

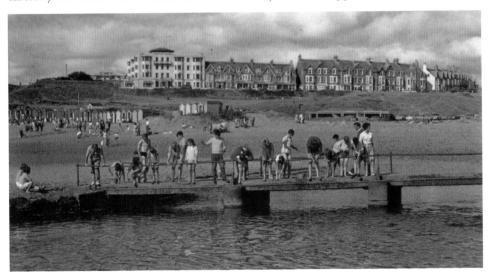

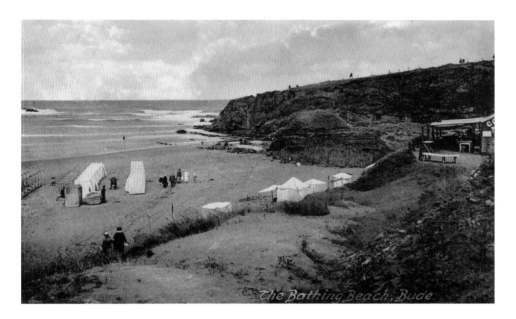

Summerleaze

A Frith postcard of Summerleaze, from 1913, this shows the bathing beach at Bude. Summerleaze probably remains Bude's most popular beach. It is but five minutes from the town centre, sandy, and with coloured boats, great surfing, the sea pool, and fabulous views. It also has Life's a Beach café with a good reputation for both food and a stunning panorama. Before the now iconic Bude Sea Pool was built, at a cost of £4,500, in the 1930s, people used to opt for safe bathing in one of the many 'pits' to be found on Summerleaze Beach. The pool was built in Saturday's Pit Bay area, but Monday's Pit was where the sluice gate from the pool now empties. Col Thynne contributed more than half to the original cost of the Bude Sea Pool, so we have much to thank him for, the sea pool being a much-loved structure in modern-day Bude.

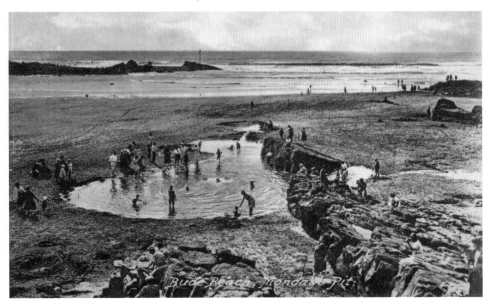

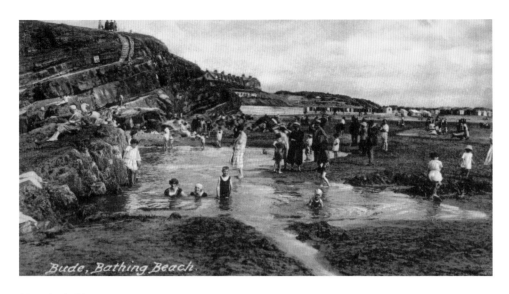

Bude, Bathing Beach.

Monday's Pit

Another view of Monday's Pit, 1926. As you can see, it was highly popular, and deep enough in parts for children to sit in up to their necks, though probably not much use for serious swimming. It was, however, safer than the current and rip tides which affect the coast, although we do now have wonderful RNLI lifeguards during peak season to help people keep safe. Of course, by the 1930s we had the outdoor swimming pool. Now, we have a great inland, warm, indoor pool called Splash, built in 1990 and refurbished in 2010, but in the 1930s it was amazing to have a new bathing pool in the great outdoors at Bude. It is still admired by many, loved by even more, and attracts locals and visitors, plus is used for many training and charity events. So-called wild and outdoor swimming now attracts many people to Bude Sea Pool as a healthy alternative. Many feel a pool washed by the tides, with spectacular views, is far preferable to chlorine. It is indeed a spectacular sight, literally a community asset, and a huge bonus for Bude.

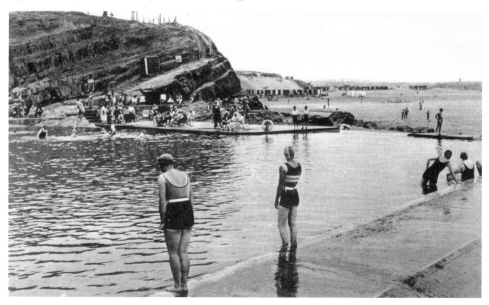

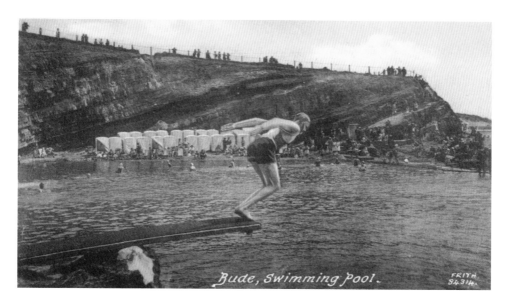

Bude, Swimming Pool.

FRITH
84314.

Bude Sea Pool

Diving at Bude Sea Pool, 1931. This would definitely be inadvisable now; anyway, there is no diving board at the pool, though this looks rather makeshift, rather than official. See the changing huts in the background. The sea pool now has some rather elegant and well-tended beach huts, but certainly fewer than are shown here. Diving is expressly prohibited at the pool, so please do not try it. However, the Save the Bude Sea Pool fundraising is ongoing, so any support (check out the website) is appreciated. From 1932, we have a lovely seaside shot of Bude Sea Pool, epitomising summer, with the ladies wearing their frocks and hats and carrying their parasols, on what is obviously a beautifully sunny day in Bude. This is not too surprising as Bude often achieves high levels of sunshine compared to the rest of the UK. The gents are standing around in their sports jackets and slacks watching the swimmers, with the more adventurous taking the waters in their bathers.

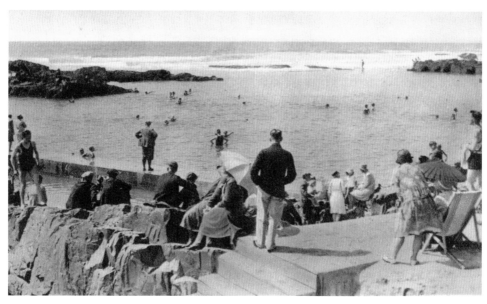

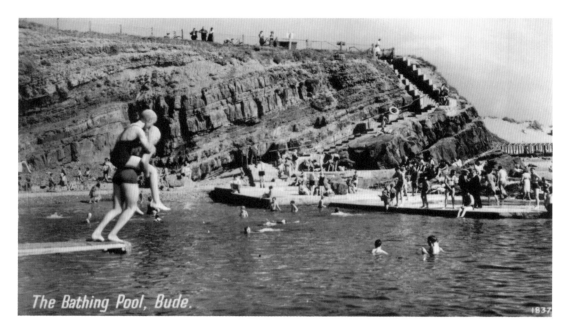

The Bathing Pool, Bude.

Bude Sea Pool Diving Board

Here we have Bude Sea Pool Diving Board, from 1949. Not only diving but piggyback diving here. Current guidelines are not to dive at the pool, as it is never certain how deep it is. Now, children learn to improve their swimming here through an annual Swim Safe scheme, and a regular fundraiser to maintain the pool is now the so-called Cross Channel Swim by relay in the sea pool. Life-saving skills are also taught in the pool. It is indispensable. Before the pool, in 1923, here is a card of Summerleaze, with a wonderful view of the Breakwater and Chapel Rock (*below*). In this image, Summerleaze retains Monday's Pit and the portable beach huts for modesty. It is a view one never tires of, and which lends a great deal of scope for exploration if prepared to walk and check out the scenery.

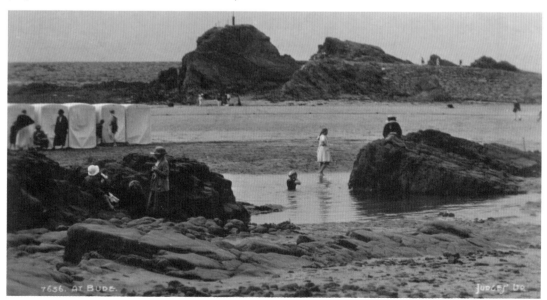

7636. AT BUDE.

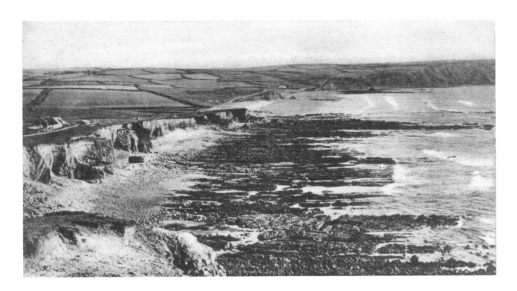

Widemouth Bay

Here we have a card of Widemouth Bay, near Bude, from 1899. Widemouth Bay (*Porth an Men*, in Cornish) is south of Bude. A popular bay, great for surfing and with many rock pools, it now also contains cafés, tea rooms, and hotels. Here, in 1899, you can see it is barely inhabited. Steeped in secrecy, the area was known for smuggling due to many rocky inlets and coves nearby, and also for submarine telecommunication cables – quite handy for GCHQ Bude to monitor transatlantic communication. The second card shows Widemouth Bay in the 1930s (*below*). You can begin to see some buildings appearing, some worryingly by the Carboniferous cliff edge, but most away from the cliffs. Many of the buildings are holiday accommodation and second homes but the view of Widemouth Bay remains special, and the bay is considered good for surfing and bodyboarding, with spectacular views from the road and upper car park, and of course, the coastal footpath, plus a decent expanse of sand. In the past, the bay was used by sloops from Wales to carry coal and limestone to the area, returning with granite, tin and copper.

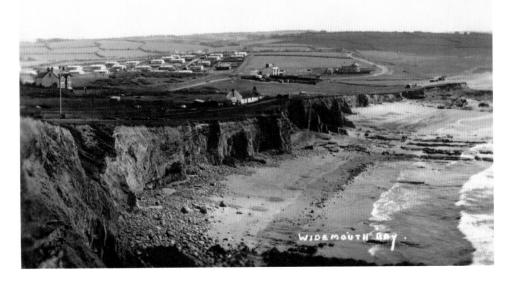

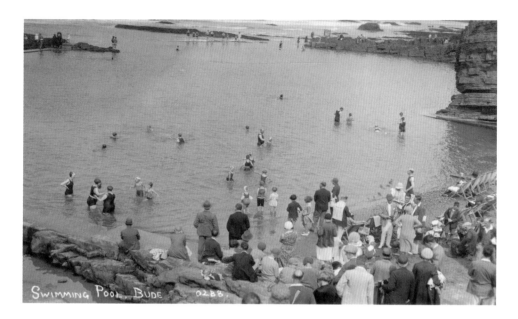

Bude Sea Pool and Bude from Efford Down

Swimming pool, 1930s. The Bude Sea Pool again, with lots of people huddled around the shallower edges and some braver people going in, including children. Note the many swimming caps worn by the women as hairdo protection. Never flattering, they had become fashionable in the 1920s when the cloche hat fashion was popular. During the Second World War, though, they took a bit of a dive in popularity when latex (rubber) was needed for war materials, only for swimming caps to resurface in the 1950s when floral hats were de rigeur. We also have Bude from Efford Down, 1890s (*below*). Although this rather resembles a Lowry drawing, this was a postcard of Bude from Efford Down, which rises from the coastal path by the Breakwater, and along to Compass Point and beyond. Always great for walking and panoramic views, but now also a popular haunt of youngsters escaping the crowds, especially in the summer.

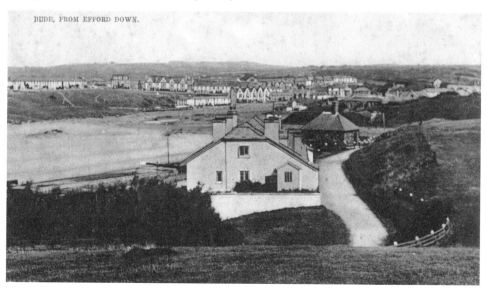

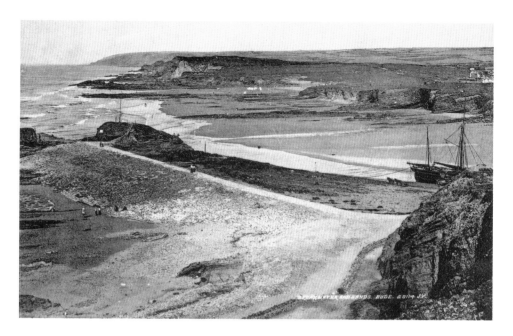

The Breakwater

This 1894 photograph of the Breakwater shows the construction at low tide. A ketch resting in the harbour has horses and carts in attendance to receive her cargo. In the background, development is just starting at Crooklets, with the stone wall just built, although the only structures are changing tents on the beach. Bude is still pretty uninhabited at this time. The second image below is the Breakwater at Bude, also from the 1890s and shows the *Lady of the Lake* ketch sailing. The ketch was built in Bideford across the Devon border, in 1862, and owned in Bude. She was wrecked on Bude sands in 1898 while carrying coal from Newport to Bude.

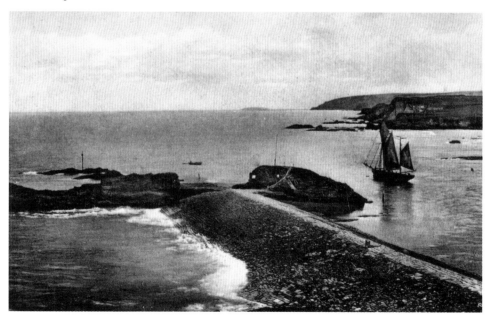

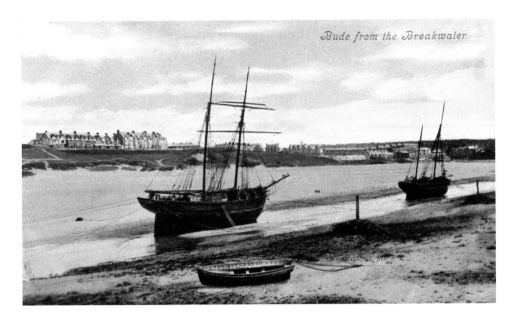

Bude from the Breakwater

The Breakwater and the Harbour

The Breakwater is a more secluded part of Bude, built to shelter the harbour from the pounding of the mighty Atlantic. At the end of the Breakwater lies Barrel Rock, the metal support for which was the propeller shaft of the stricken ship, the SS *Belem*, wrecked at Northcott Mouth, in 1919. Bude has traditionally found uses for anything lost at sea, from wrecks, and more recently from beach cleans, where plastic debris washed up on shore is often used to make art, although locals would prefer to stick to driftwood. Marine life is sadly also washed up, including sea birds, a whale and seals, which take a pounding in rough seas. The harbour in the 1900s shows the 73-ton schooner *Annie Davey*, which was built in Stapleton's yard on Bude Canal in 1873, along with the ketch *Lady Acland*, which was taken out of the water several times for repairs. In 1904, the *Lady Acland* was renamed *Agnes*, after Her Ladyship's daughter. She continued to sail through the Second World War, surviving until 1955 when she was wrecked off the West Indies.

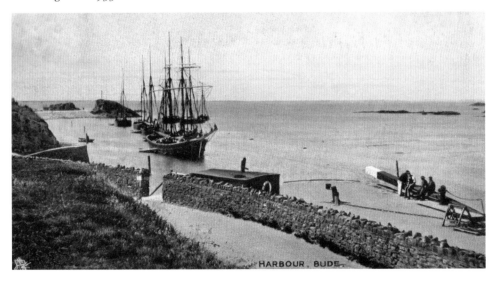

HARBOUR, BUDE.

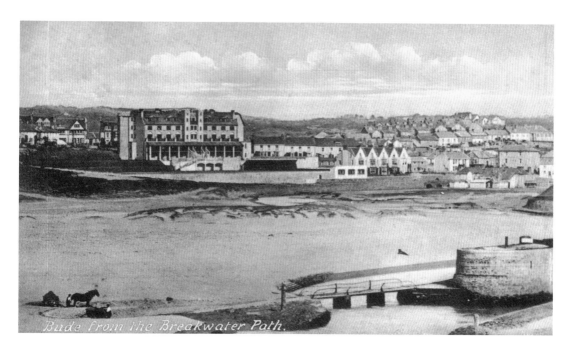

Bude from the Breakwater Path.

The Breakwater

You do get a fabulous view of Bude across Summerleaze from the coast path – known on this card as the Breakwater Path – above the Breakwater. The above card comes from around 1910. You can see the Grenville Hotel dominating the skyline, plus the lock gates and Nanny Moore's Bridge, which looks much more insignificant from this angle. The coloured image is of Bude's Chapel Rock at the Breakwater, taken in 1893. For some reason the rock is without its flagstaff here. Despite the Breakwater, entry to the harbour was still hazardous due to rough seas and awkward tides. The stone flags could be rather slippy, too. The chapel was dedicated to St Michael, and was originally occupied by a hermit who kept a fire burning to guide mariners to safe haven – hence Bede's Haven.

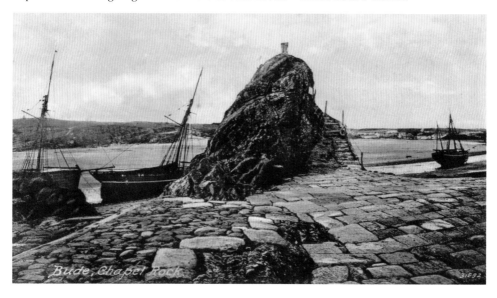

Bude, Chapel Rock.

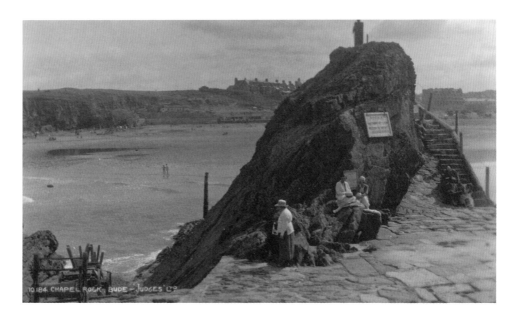

Chapel Rock

Chapel Rock became a major landmark for visitors to Bude, though the Breakwater is still an area that, while popular with locals, many visitors miss because it is not readily accessible by car. See the notice about bathing at 'low watch' on this Judges card from 1927 (*above*). The ladies on the rocks seem to be enjoying their peace and quiet. One has even taken her hat off! Meanwhile, had you been at Chapel Rock in 1896, you might have seen the two-masted ketch *Friendship*, and the smack (a traditional fishing boat) called the *Boconnoc*. What a delightful sight that would have been. Fishing was not very commercially viable in Bude, so there was never a large community of fishermen, unlike some other Cornish coastal towns. The coast was too rugged and the waters rough, but farmers went to sea when large shoals of mackerel or pilchards arrived, and fish were smoked or pickled in the fish cellars to sustain them through the leaner times.

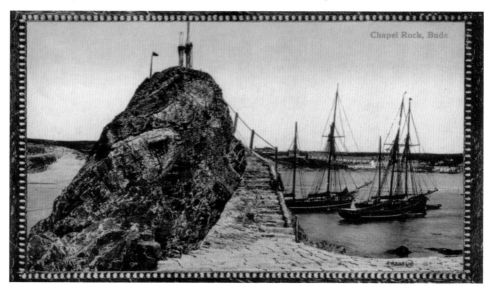

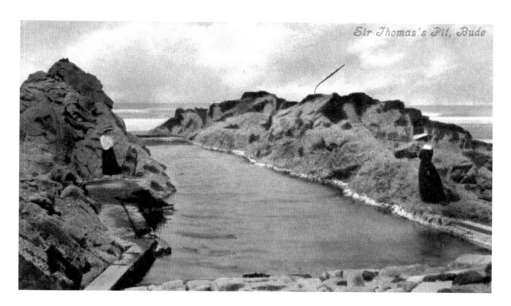

Sir Thomas's Pit, Bude

Tommy's Pit

Tommy's Pit is a dearly beloved spot for many. This hand-coloured card above dates from around 1890, and it is called the rather grander Sir Thomas's Pit, named after the swimming pool of Thomas Acland. How the women got onto the often slippy rocks in those skirts is anyone's guess, given the conditions were rather windswept. In the background, the pole on Barrel Rock was bent over and replaced a few years later. Fast forward to the 1920s and we see people actually swimming in Tommy's Pit, a rock pool that is still used today; it was constructed in 1859 as a graduated depth bathing pool for gentlemen. Bathers paid tuppence a swim and were fined a penny if caught swimming naked. This little ditty explains it all, though not sure any of the men would have tried it with the ladies present: 'There once was a young man from Bude / Who fancied a dip in the nude / For a thruppenny bit / He could swim in Tom's Pit / Which included the fine for being rude!'

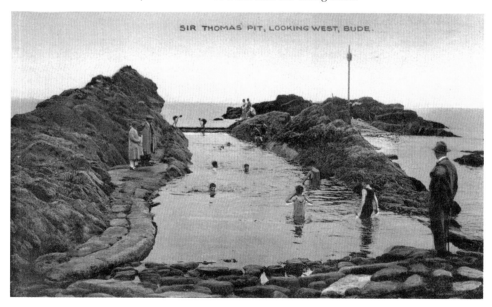

SIR THOMAS PIT, LOOKING WEST, BUDE.

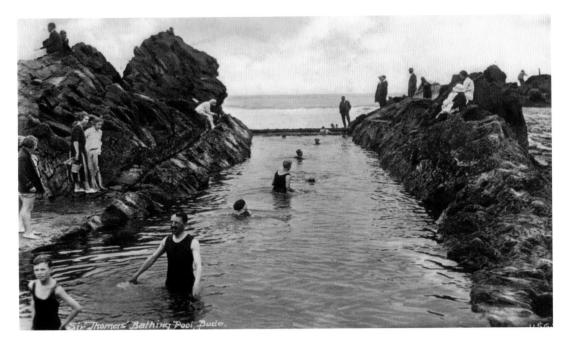

Tommy's Pit and the Iron Bridge

This view of Tommy's Pit is wonderful, giving a real feel for the fashions of the day, including the moustaches. Taken in 1923, there seem to be ladies swimming in here, too. At high tide, the pool is not usable, as it would be very easy to be swept out to sea, or smashed against the rocks. Sir Thomas's son compiled the first tide tables and placed a half-tide cross at the end of Coach Rock at Summerleaze. At the harbour, the iron bridge was originally built to carry the wagons, which traversed an extensive system of rails – much of which now lies beneath Summerleaze Beach, bringing sand to the waiting tub boats on the canal. Now people use it to cross the river at low tide; at high tide it is usually covered. In the past, there was a rowing boat service run by Capt. Brinton to make the crossing, but now you either get very wet or walk round the long way.

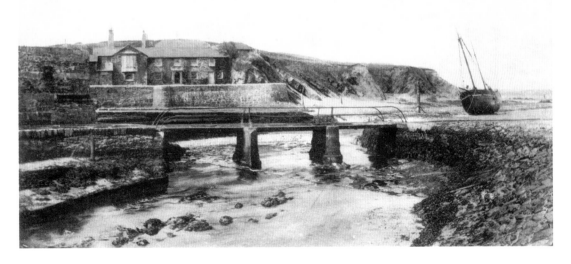

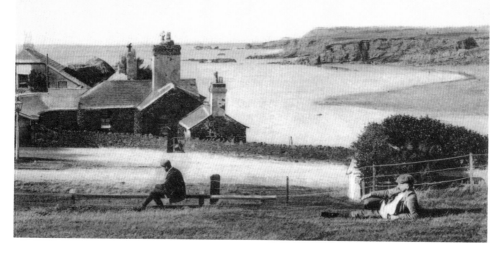

Harbour Entrance

The beach from the harbour entrance is close to Efford Cottage. The gentlemen here are carefully posed for the scene. Some feel that Efford would have been an appropriate name for Bude; it certainly has a historic feel, but it is hard to imagine Bude as anything else now. Efford Cottage was rebuilt from old fish cellars and various members of the Acland family stayed there, including Sir Thomas who would arrived on his yacht, The *Lady of St Kilda*. The Bude Breakwater was built between 1839 and 1843; it is now Grade II listed. The Breakwater is a popular place to walk, but waves wash over it at high tide, and dramatic rescues have been known. We no longer see double-masted ketches in the harbour, nor single-masted smacks, but some occasional fishing boats and pleasure boats may usually be seen in the water.

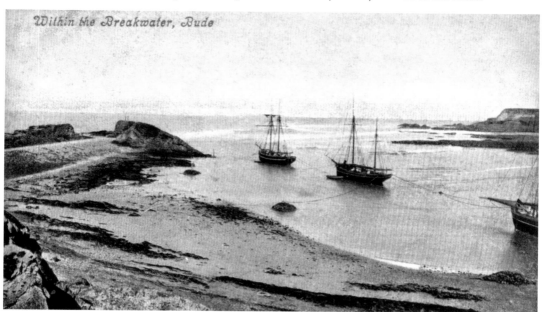

Within the Breakwater, Bude

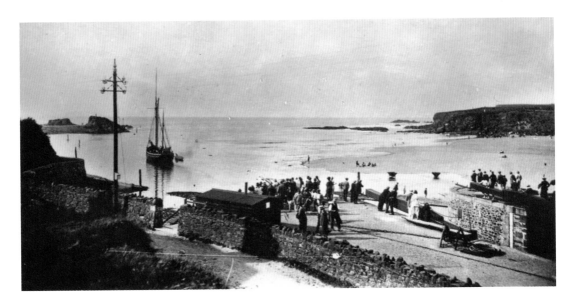

The Locks and Efford Cottage

This rather nice, clear card above came from Lilywhite Ltd of Sowerby Bridge, Yorkshire, dating back to 1910. It shows people watching the boats leaving the locks. There is always something fascinating about watching boats leaving and arriving, so you can imagine this small crowd gathering to see these ones off. A trade did grow in shipping groceries to Bristol (not sure if that included pasties), while limestone and coal was brought to Bude from South Wales. Neighbouring Efford Cottage did not always have its pink exterior. Indeed, originally it was a dilapidated thatched cottage, a site of fish cellars and lime kilns. Here, the boats, Stucley and Alford, are nearby.

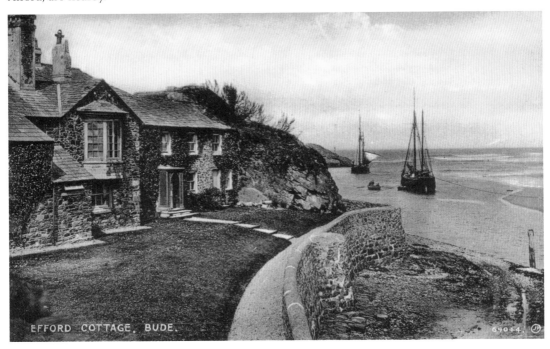

EFFORD COTTAGE, BUDE.

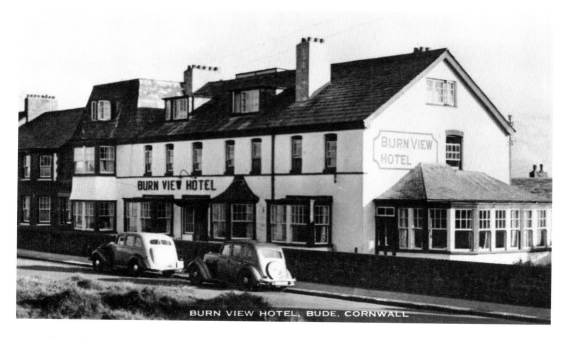

Burn View Hotel and Grenville Hotel

Burn View Hotel is featured on this card, complete with rather lovely old cars parked outside. Another of Bude's disappeared hotels, the Burn View Hotel is seen here in the 1940s. It was later renamed Burn Court Hotel and was situated near the golf club. Burn View, Queen Street and Morwenna terrace were developed by the Thynne family, from red brick brought in by the railway. The rather more imposing image of the Grenville Hotel dates from the 1930s. At five storeys high, the hotel was (and remains, although changed in usage) castellated in appearance, but the whole somehow looks a little discordant and disparate. It is not Bude's prettiest building but it may be its most commanding.

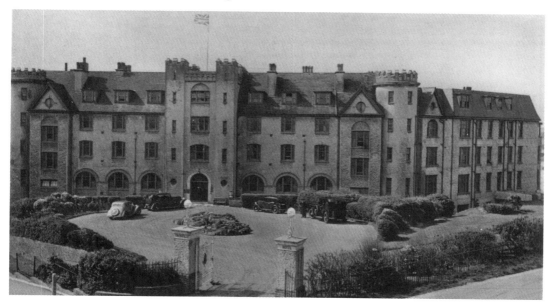

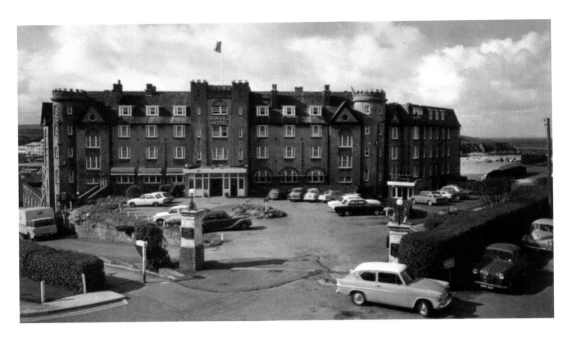

Grenville Hotel

This postcard of the Grenville Hotel in the 1970s (*above*) has a veritable display of English cars that are no longer available, so I had to take a car enthusiast's advice on this one. In the foreground is a Ford Anglia. To the furthest right of that is a Morris Minor and there is a green Hillman Imp on the grass. To the right of the pink one looks to be a Wolseley, and to the left is either a Morris or Austin. To the right of it appears to be a Triumph, and there may be the odd Dolomite in there. The luxury model in the middle could be a Bentley or Rolls. Interestingly, the car behind that has black-and-white wheels, very popular in the USA and not popular in the UK. Back in the 1900s, the Grenville described itself as the largest and only modern equipped hotel in Bude fronting the Atlantic. Both the Grenville and the Falcon stayed open all year, so were not seasonal. Later, many other private properties were converted into smaller hotels, such as the Victorian Efford Down House and Hartland House.

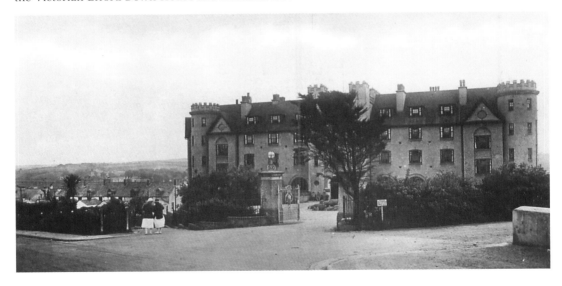

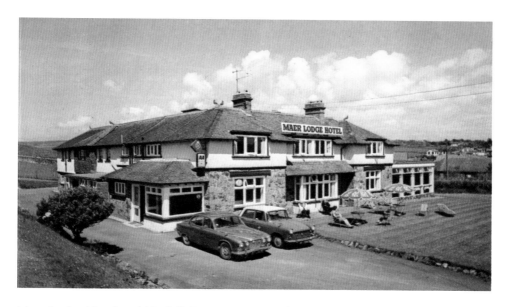

Maer Lodge Hotel and Norfolk Temperance Hotel

Maer Lodge Hotel was built in the early 1900s, and seen here in the 1960s; the hotel gave way to a small housing estate development, so no longer exists. There are now closer hotels to Crooklets Beach, such as the modern, family-friendly Tommy Jack's. The Norfolk Temperance Hotel in the early 1900s also features here. The Temperance Movement urged moderation in alcohol consumption, occasionally to the point of teetotalism, and obviously attracted enough people to the cause to have a 'dry house' for abstainers situated in Bude. Wesley's Methodism was popular in Cornwall and also strongly associated with Temperance, so maybe that is why the hotel was built. Originally, Temperance was to dissuade people from drinking strong spirits, rather than wine and beer, but later teetotalism was advocated. Not sure why it was called the Norfolk though.

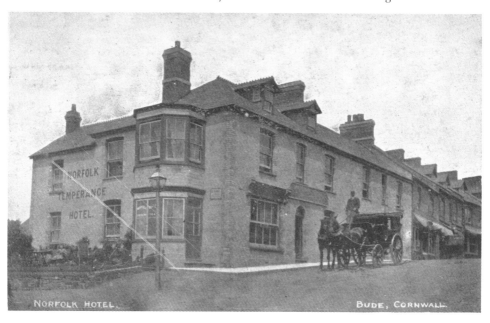

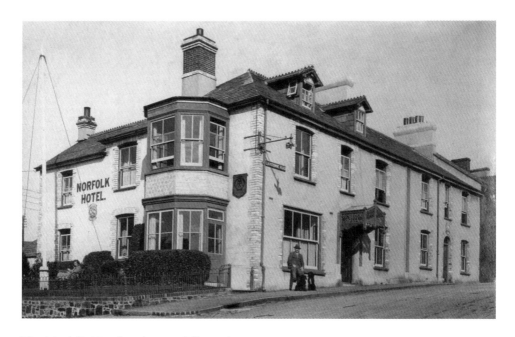

The Norfolk Hotel and Westcliff Hotel

The Norfolk Hotel had moved on in the 1920s, when the Temperance Movement had lost its popularity and momentum. Visitors to the Norfolk could still enjoy the genteel activities of bowling and croquet, so maybe it appealed to a specific kind of customer. In 1938, Westcliff House, at the end of Summerleaze Crescent (though it is not crescent shaped), was converted into the Westcliff Hotel, which is seen here in its heyday in the 1950s (*below*). It has now suffered the fate of so many others of Bude's hotels and been converted into flats, but it must be said, they are stunningly situated. Other hotels, many with fine restaurants, have sprung up on Summerleaze Crescent, including The Edgcumbe, The Grosvenor, The Beach and Atlantic House.

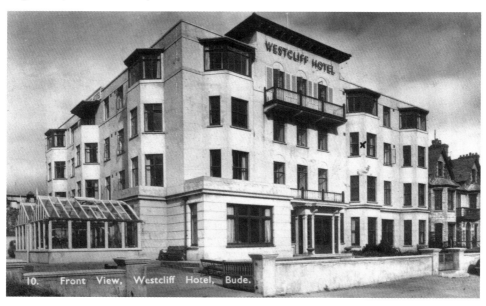

10. Front View, Westcliff Hotel, Bude.

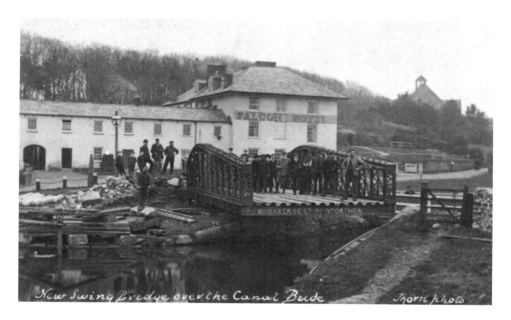

Falcon New Swing Bridge and the Falcon Hotel

From 1906, this view of the Falcon New Swing Bridge above shows the opening of the new swing bridge over the canal, with the Falcon Hotel still without its tower in the background. This bridge was opened to permit ships to discharge at the warehouses of the upper basin and was itself replaced in 1962 by the present, fixed bridge. The wooden swing bridge over the canal led to the new road, The Crescent, across the marshes, terminating in a bridge (Bencoolen) and a toll house. Meanwhile, at the other side of town, across the canal, this postcard below shows the Falcon Hotel, completed with a newly constructed swing bridge, open for shipping and also rather impressive looking. Many locals remember walking across it. It would be lovely to have something like it still there, as it has a certain character.

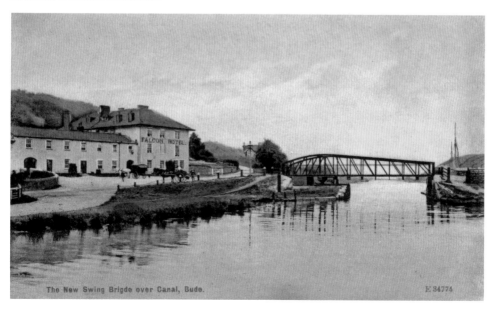

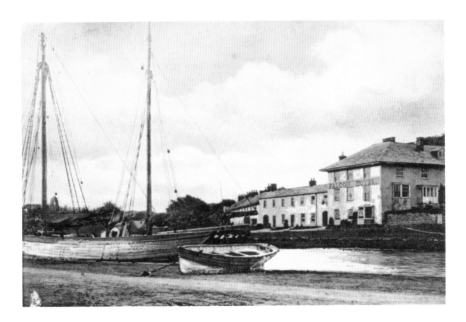

The Falcon Hotel

The Falcon was established in 1798 as accommodation (a lodging house) for captains of merchant vessels. Since then, the hotel has continued to thrive as the Falcon Crest Inn, and then, from 1826, as one of Bude's premier hotels. It was once visited by Alfred, Lord Tennyson, who famously broke his leg here in 1848 when he fell over a garden wall, spending his convalescence in Bude. Conversely, a clergyman, Canon Maskell described it (rather unfairly, in my view) as 'pretentious'. The Falcon was named as such as a falcon forms part of the Acland family crest (the Aclands were patrons). This view below is from 1903, accompanied by one of the Falcon in the 1920s. The Falcon was, and remains, an idyllic venue, close to the canal for rowing boats, the beach at Summerleaze, and the Breakwater. The Breakwater was and is a popular spot. Originally, it was constructed to stand 10 feet above the spring tide levels and connect Chapel Rock with the mainland.

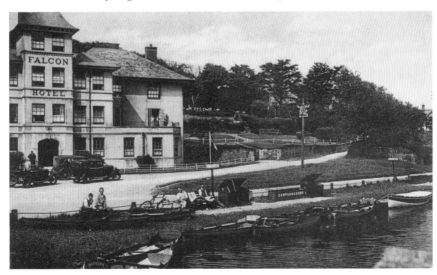

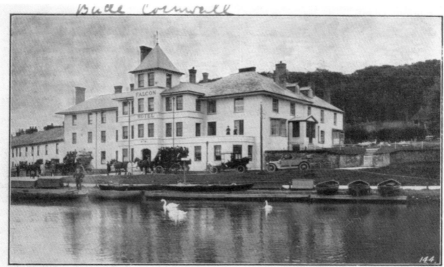

Bude Cornwall

Free Golf (Sunday play) to Visitors staying in the Hotel.   Free Garage.   Moderate Terms.

The Falcon Hotel

By 1915, the Falcon offered free golf to visitors on Sundays, and a free garage, so you can see how important the car was becoming. As you can see, the sender has written on where the hotel is, as while it describes all the plus points, including moderate terms, the postcard fails to locate the building. In season, Bude offered croquet, tennis, cricket and golf, so was a great place for healthy outdoor holidays. It is still a healthy outdoor holiday venue though croquet is no longer offered. In 1905, the Falcon is pictured here with carriages and horses. The Falcon described itself as a family hotel, nearest to the sea, even then with free golf for visitors on Maer Down (course now abandoned), with the advantage that an omnibus met all trains.

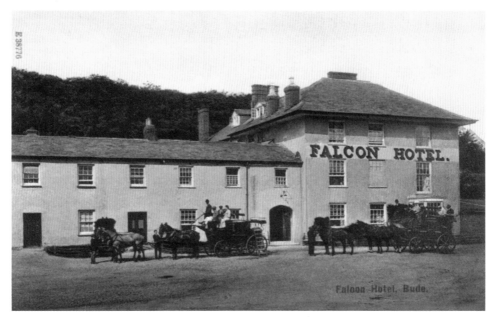

Falcon Hotel, Bude.

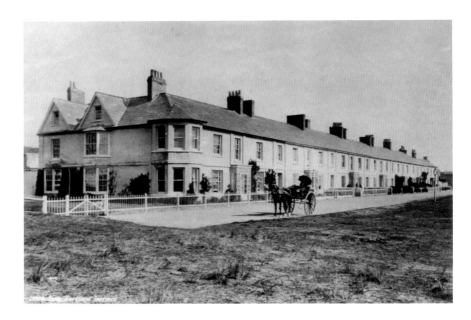

Hartland Terrace and the Headland Pavilion

This view of Hartland Terrace above, in 1890, is a Francis Frith card. There is a pony and trap outside Hartland House, once the summer residence of the Bristol Fry family (manufacturers of chocolate) who used to visit Bude on their yacht *Fireflash*. The building was later converted to the Hartland Hotel and is currently being converted again, to be known as the Base, ideally situated for the beaches, town, and coastal path. In the 1930s, the Headland Pavilion was the place to go for a dance, for it was built as a 'dance café' behind Summerleaze Crescent (despite local objections). It catered for major coach tours and was one of the few developments on the Down at this time. According to local historians, Bere and Dudley Stamp, the owners handed out free milkshakes to children at the time of the Coronation in 1937, which was a great marketing success. Now it is being developed into more flats, called Atlantic Rise.

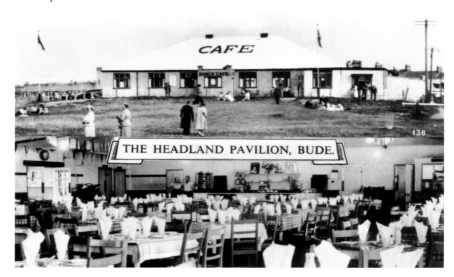

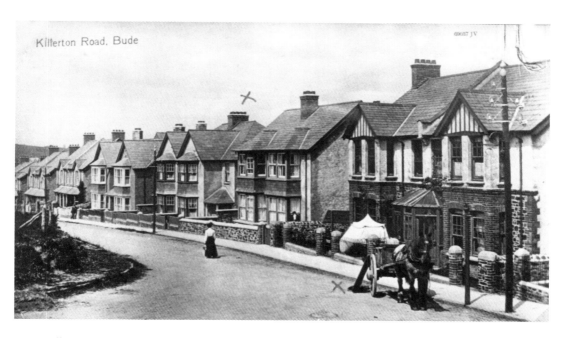

Killerton Road, Bude

Killerton Road and Queen Street

Killerton Road is not exactly the town's centre, but nor is it outskirts; it now primarily comprises housing. A delivery horse and cart is on the hill in this card, from 1911. At this time, only one side of the road was developed. The road used to be called Tagg's Lane, as the sheep track to Stratton, and was part of an Acland family housing development. From a similar period, we have Queen Street in Bude, taken in the 1910s. As you can see, much of Queen Street at this time was residential, whereas now it is part of the commercial area of Bude, with both sides of the street lined with shops and cafés. Bath chairs (three wheeled devices to carry the sick or elderly) were once available for hire on Queen Street from Maynard's.

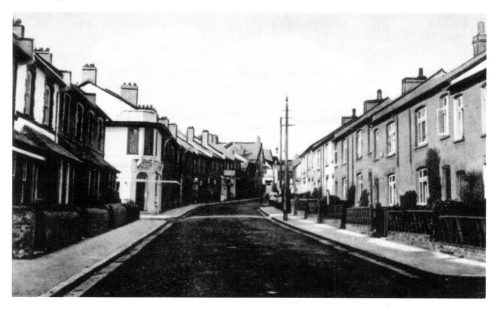

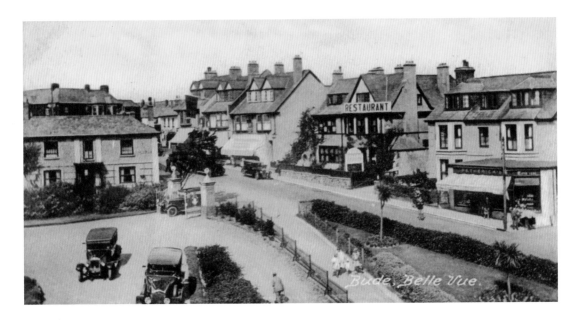

The Triangle

Meanwhile, we have Belle Vue (*above*), which looks rather grand here, with its restaurants and stores, including Petherick's. This view is from 1929, taken from the Grenville Hotel. The building in the centre with the word restaurant was the Grosvenor Hotel and Restaurant and is where Time & Tide and Grosvenor Mansions flats are now. On the right is Petherick's china and bookshop, where Boots now is. See the little girls with their pram here by the Granville Tea Rooms in 1915? You can also see the Grenville Hotel plus its original garage alongside the road to Summerleaze. By now, the Triangle boasted the Granville Tea Rooms, also known as Windsor House. The tea rooms were leased from Algernon Carteret Thynne of Penstowe, Kilkhampton, esq. to a lady called Lilian Laloe, records interestingly held across the Tamar in the North Devon Records Office. Not many people around in this image below, but this was during the First World War.

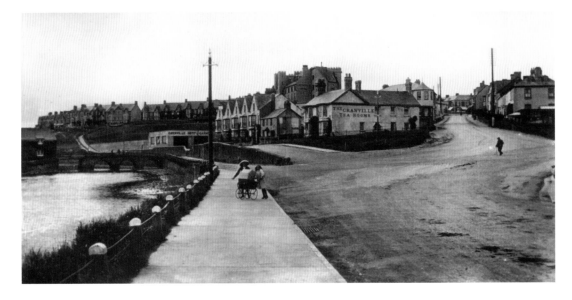

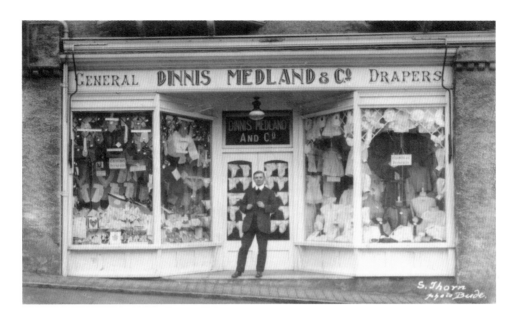

Belle Vue and Bude Cinema

Dinnis Medland's Shop, Bude. This shot shows Dinnis Medland in front of his shop (which is now still a clothes shop but owned by national chain Fat Face) in Belle Vue, and was taken at Christmas (there are adverts for Christmas presents in the window) sometime in the 1910s. This shop sold ladies' and children's clothing; according to the 1910 Bude guide, he had another shop, selling gentlemen's clothing and household linen, in the Strand. The original Bude cinema, at the end of Burn View, was built in 1920 and replaced by the new Picture House on Summerleaze Down in 1935. The advertised film is *The Kid*, starring Charlie Chaplin, which was released in 1921. The first film is said to have been *The Ten Commandments*, with a Mr Moffatt at the piano. Bude no longer has a cinema, except for the wonderful independent cinema, The Rebel, 5 miles down the A39 at Poundstock.

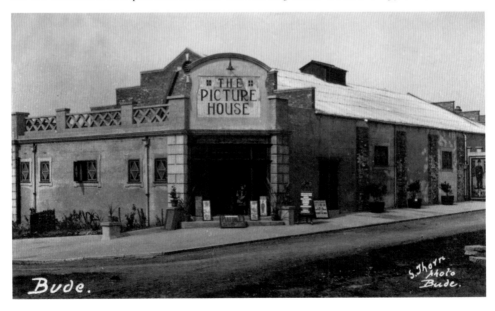

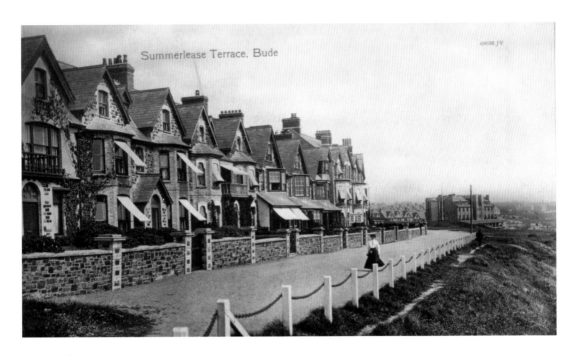

Summerleaze Crescent

Summerleaze Crescent, Bude, is shown here in 1914. I love Summerleaze Crescent because it leads you directly to the coast path above the sea pool, and the Down, while also affording easy access to the top end of Belle Vue and a great view to the sea. Though this rather elegant lady would not agree, sitting eating a pasty in the sunshine on the grass here is one of life's pleasures, as is afternoon tea with friends at one of the many hotel restaurants. Summerleaze Crescent in 1911 (*below*) is appropriately called Beach Terrace here. This is the end that leads off from Belle Vue. The terrace is now something on a hotel area, with bars, cafés and restaurants catering for all tastes and pockets.

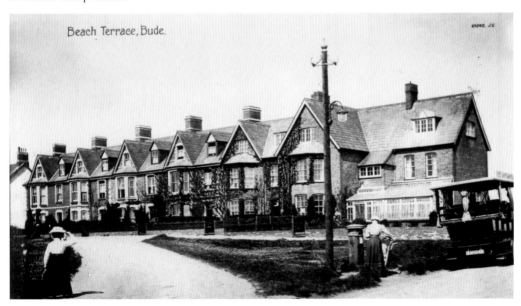

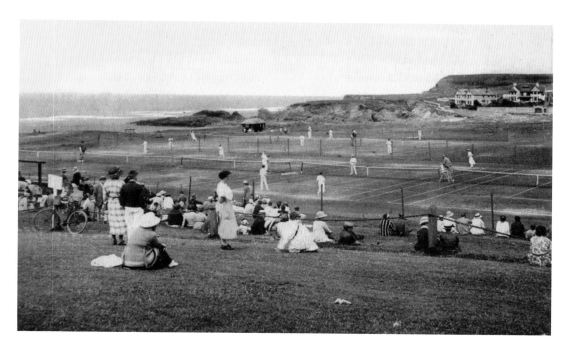

Tennis Club

Summerleaze Lawn Tennis Club is featured here in the 1920s. Bude Tennis Club is now situated at the Recreation Ground at Levens Terrace, but the cricket club, with an impressive and relatively new pavilion, is still sited here. Called one of the most picturesque cricket grounds in the world, the view is hard to beat. Back in the '20s, both sports were enjoyed here. It is maybe a little breezy for tennis though, so the new site is probably better.

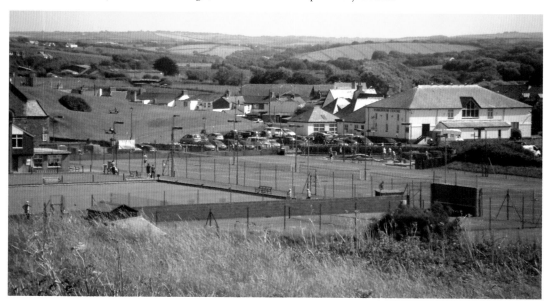

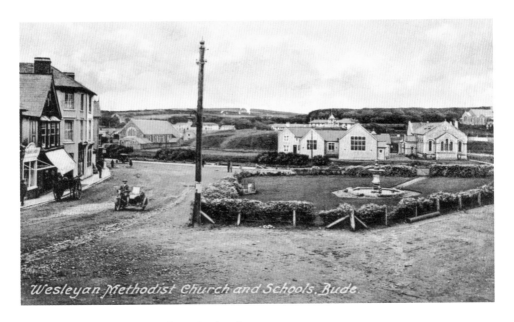

Wesleyan Methodist Church and Schools

Wesleyan Methodist Church and Schools

Wesleyan Methodist church and schools are seen from here the Triangle in the 1910s. The Thynne family was staunchly Anglican, and never allowed a Nonconformist chapel on their land, but the Aclands (also Anglican) were more tolerant. The nineteenth-century landowners (and, indeed, The Revd Hawker of Morwenstow) were very hostile to Wesley's Methodism, but the current Methodist church was built in 1890, and Killerton Road boasted a United Reformed church, while the Roman Catholics were served in Bencoolen Road, so there was a variety of worship in the town. Many Wesleyan Methodist chapels have long since been converted to holiday homes. The Wesleyans were the original Methodists, the church founded by John Wesley in the eighteenth century; they were very strong in Cornwall, including Bude.

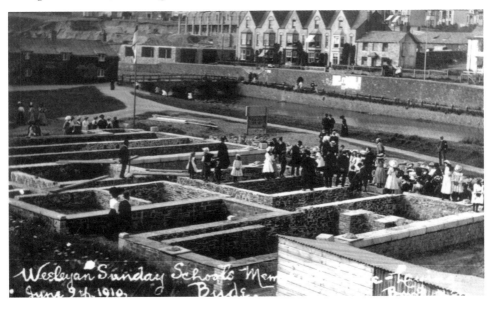

Wesleyan Sunday Schools Mem... June 9th 1910. Bude.

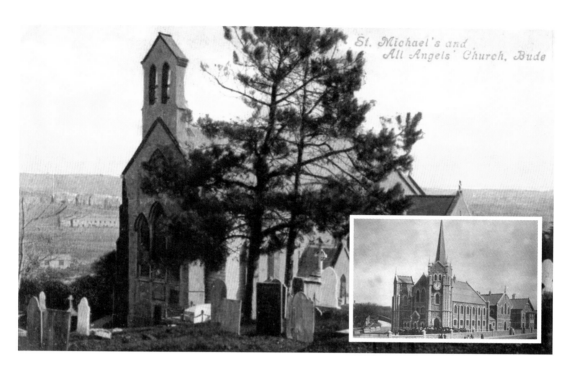

St. Michael's and All Angels' Church, Bude

Flexbury

Flexbury chapel's opening is featured here. Flexbury once formed part of the manor of Poughill which later became known as Broomhill. Various parts of the area, such as Maer and Flexbury were then sold off. For almost 400 years, Bude was owned by two major families, the Arundels (later the Aclands) on one side of the river and the Grenvilles/Thynnes on the other side. They seemed to be largely on good terms and inter-married. There is a rumour that the spire of the church was built as a rude gesture, but we will never know the truth of that. Conversely, St Michael's and All Angels' church is on the southern side of the harbour and looks above Bude. It is now the town's parish church, consecrated on 29 September, 1895. The church stone came from Trerice near Newlyn. Built by the Acland family, it is a Grade II listed building, with a turret containing two bells and a clock. The original church was served by Stratton's John Skinner King who tended to be notoriously rather late for his services. The first vicar was Revd J. S. Avery of Ebbingford Vicarage. On a different note, the churchyard is the burial place of Pamela (Pixie) Colman-Smith, designer of the Waite-Smith divinatory tarot cards. She died in penury and was buried here, presumably in an unmarked grave, in 1951.

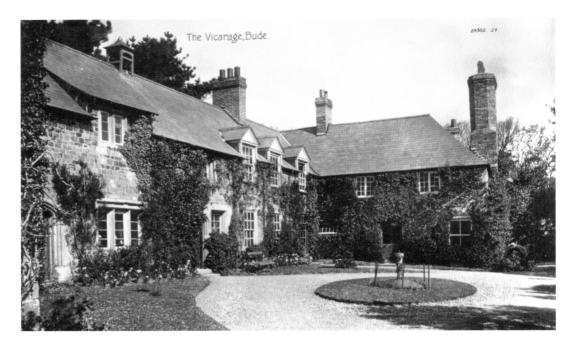

The Vicarage, Bude.

Ebbingford

Ebbingford or Efford (Vicarage), Bude, is shown here in 1896. Ebbingford Manor is a Grade II listed building, which was inhabited by local historian Bryan Dudley Stamp. It dates as far back as 1183. Daphne du Maurier is said to have visited the house, as did eccentric Morwenstow vicar Stephen Hawker. The house has a rich history. From 1861, the house was offered to the church as a vicarage, but in 1898 it was acquired by one of the best-known twentieth-century British geographers, Sir Laurence Dudley Stamp (1898–1966) when he retired, and has stayed with the Stamp family ever since.

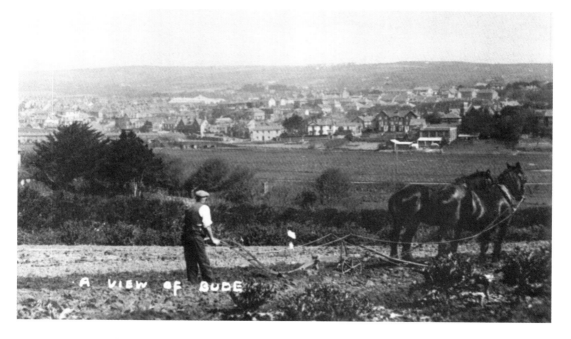

Lynstone and the Crescent

A very rural view from around 1910 (*above*). This is taken from Lynstone, which is on the Widemouth Bay road climbing from and overlooking Bude. Lynstone now has a caravan park and extensive coastal views. Below shows the Crescent, Bude, around 1920s, which was previously known as South Terrace. An old Morris convertible is the only vehicle using the Crescent in this shot from the 1920s, but now it is a main thoroughfare out past the Falcon on the climb to Widemouth Bay. The wall on the left bordered a water meadow; today's Crescent car and coach park by the Tourist Information Centre would not appear for many years, so it would then have been quite pretty.

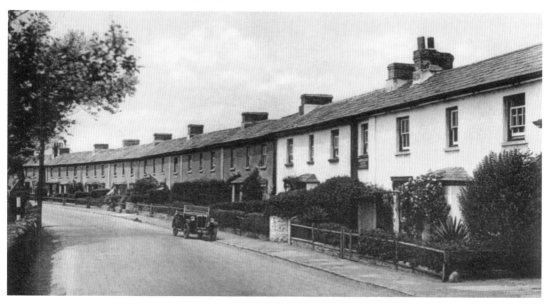

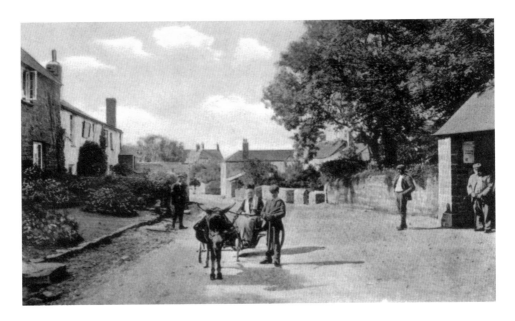

Poughill

The pretty hamlet of Poughill, 1900s. Sir Goldsworthy Gurney lived there for a time. In the Domesday Book Poughill was known as Pochelle. By 1536, it was referred to as Poghyll. The Manor of Poughill was later known as Broomhill, which it remains today. Poughill (pronounced Puffil) is seen here with St Olaf's church in the background. Olaf (995–1030) was a Norwegian king and saint, though what brought him to the attention of Poughill is mysterious. The church of St Olaf was built in the fourteenth century and extended during the fifteenth century, according to the Conservation Area appraisal. Extended building works imply prosperity at that time.

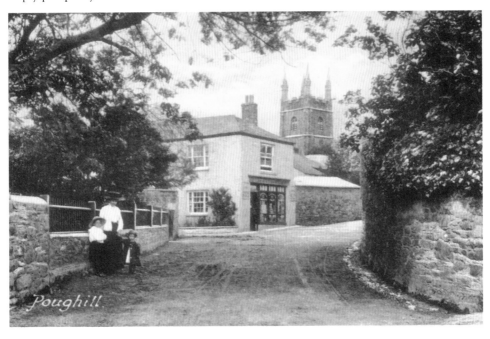

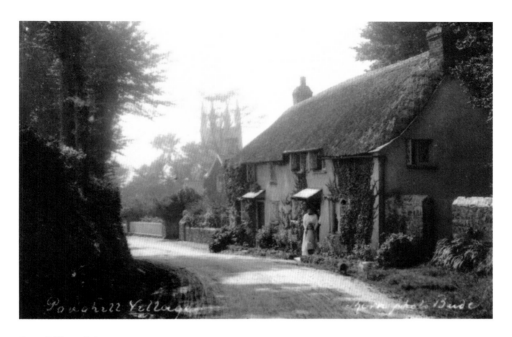

Poughill and Stratton

Poughill, 1900s. The evangelical Anglican St Olaf's church contains frescoes from around 1470, depicting St Christopher. St Olaf was King of Norway and a martyr, but now Poughill is mainly viewed by visitors as a charming rural hamlet, with lovely thatched cottages and a pub, the Preston Gate. It is also used as a back route into Bude from the A39 via Stonehill. Stratton is shown here in the 1900s (*below*). It has really not changed that much apart from the road surface and the level of traffic. Bude later gently developed, some say at the expense of Stratton, which declined in the period before the First World War.

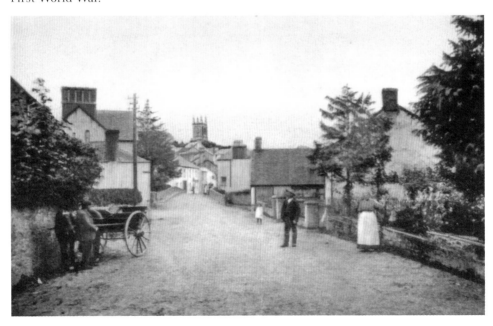

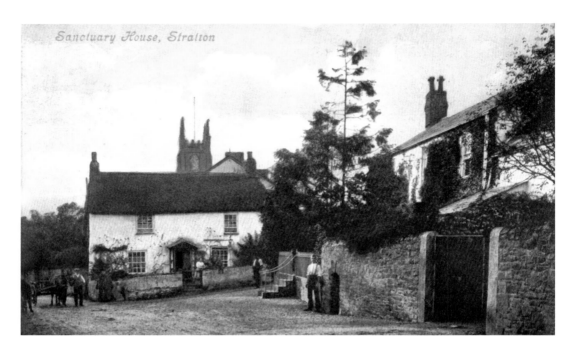

Stratton

Stratton (*Strasnedh* in Cornish) was so named because the area was, at one time, held by the monks of St Stephen's priory in Launceston. The church dominated Stratton in the late eighteenth century, but there were also more than twelve alehouses and inns, and it was a centre for justice with a jail or 'clink', police station and court. The saying goes, 'Stratton was a market town when Bude was just a furzy down.' This first image is from 1900. Stratton, the Leat, is a 1910 Frith card. A leat is an artificial watercourse or aqueduct dug into the ground, usually supplying water to a millpond or watermill.

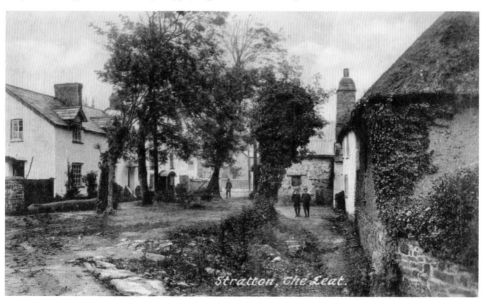

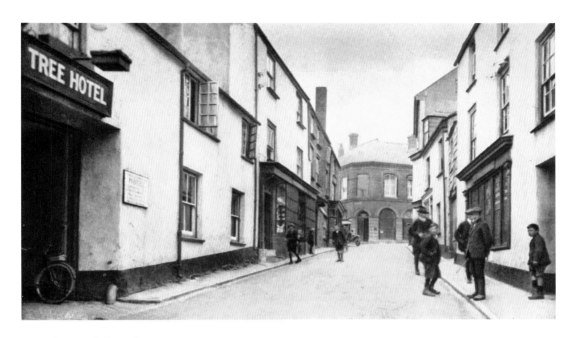

Stratton's Fore Street

Stratton's Fore Street in glorious colour, dating from around 1910 (*above*). Strat means road and ton means manor, so you can guess the meaning of Stratton, which adjoins Bude and was originally far more important. The Tree Inn (there called hotel but known as an inn since the 1790s) is still in existence; a Court Leat was held there until the 1900s as Stratton was a centre for local justice. The memorial in the square was built after the First World War. It may not look too grand here, but Leland in 1600 described Stratton as a 'prettye town'. It developed into a commercial centre, known for leather and agriculture, but was also known for garlic, which grew in the wild and was cultivated as a cure for animal diseases.

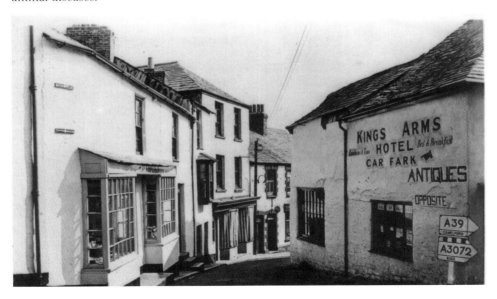

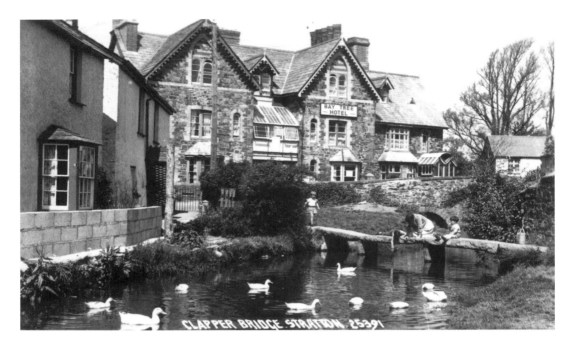

The Clapper Bridge and Church, Stratton

The Clapper Bridge, Stratton, 1950s (*above*). This card shows the Bay Tree Hotel and the Clapper Bridge. A clapper bridge is a primitive form of stone bridge, popular around Devon and usually made of long thin slabs of stone. Local children would cross the Stratton one on their way to school, whatever the weather, though most probably fell in the river at some point. It was still safer than crossing roads. The bridge was later demolished. The church, St Andrew's (*below*), is Grade I listed due to its Norman origins. Over 750 years old, the church is a focal point in Stratton, situated up a hill, so a dramatic overseer of the town. The post office and church area has been developed since this time.

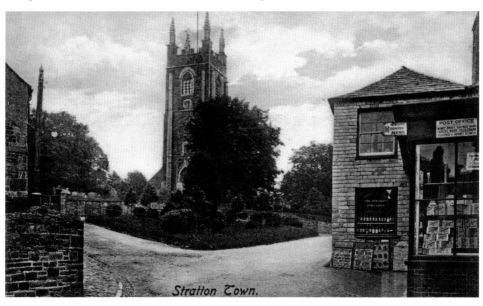

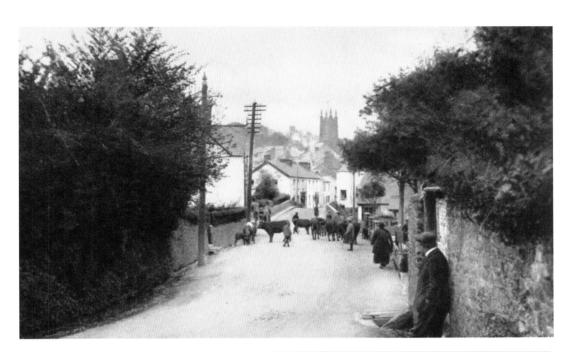

Stratton

Stratton, shown here in the 1930s, is surrounded by farmland even today. A cattle market continued in Stratton until the 1980s. Stratton feels like a village rather than a town. If all the cars were removed, it would be very much like stepping back in time, despite some development. To the right is a Francis Frith image of Stratton from 1929 where, with even limited transport, the narrow streets begin to look crowded. Sadly, Stratton now contains many second homes that are empty for much of the year. Some say the soul of the village is no longer as it was. Hard to imagine that in the eighteenth century Stratton was an important commercial centre, with not only the usual trades, but also two doctors and a druggist, plus a hatmaker and wigmaker, denoting wealth.

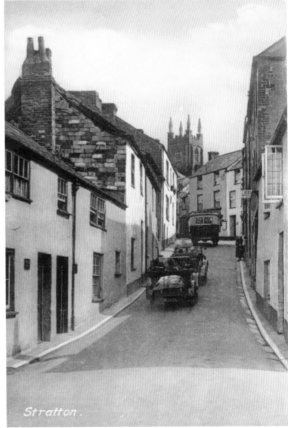

Stratton.

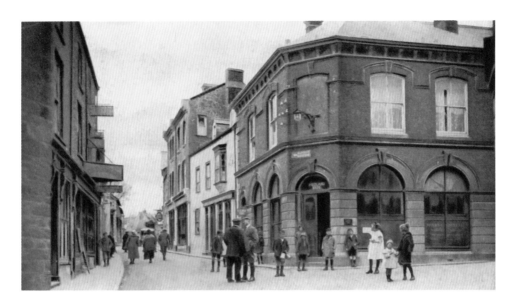

Bank Corner and St Margaret's

Bank Corner, Stratton, early 1900s (*above*). A view of the junction of Fore Street and Maiden Street in Stratton in the 1900s. Named Bank Corner because the building opposite housed a bank – although here it seems to be occupied by Medland Bros – this was one of the busier parts of the village, with many shops, now long gone. A sign on the wall, pointing the way to Bideford and Clovelly, points out that this was at that time the main route up through North Cornwall, until the Stratton bypass on the A39 was constructed; I cannot imagine all today's A39 traffic passing through this route! The second image is of St Margaret's as St Petroc's. St Petroc's was once based in Killerton Road, in what was St Margaret's Hotel. The school is now in Ocean View Road. This shot shows one of the traditional, formal schoolrooms, with wooden desks and chairs and a spartan appearance. It also served a period as a girls' school but is now a private residence.

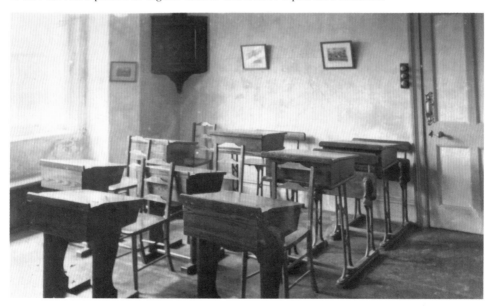

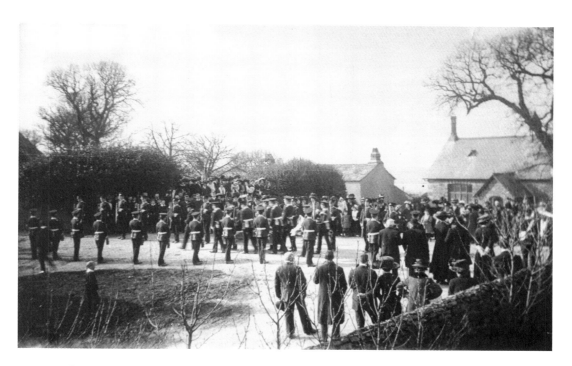

Marhamchurch

Not sure whose funeral this was, though local recollection is that it was a local campaigner. It certainly looks like a grand send off. Marhamchurch derives from the Celtic saint Marwenne (in Cornish, *Morwenna*), daughter of the Welsh King Brychan, who travelled to Cornwall in the fifth century. The hilltop village near Bude was recorded in the Domesday Book. The post office closed in 2009. It remains an attractive village, with holiday lets, a church and a pub.

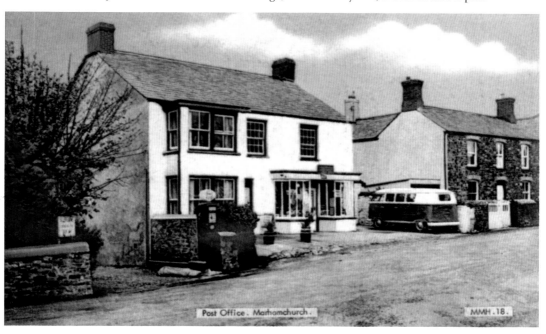

Post Office. Marhamchurch.   MMH.18.

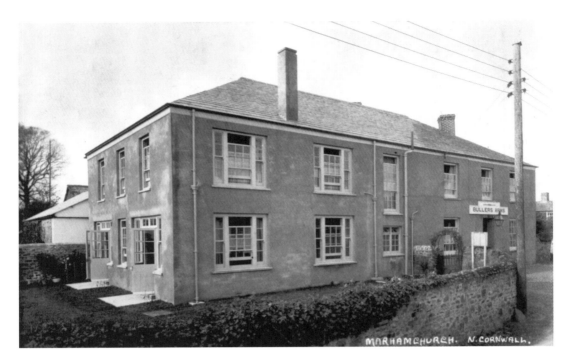

The Bullers Arms and Bude from the Air

The Bullers Arms is the pub at the heart of Marhamchurch village, near to Bude. Established around 1856, it was named after Gen. Sir Redvers Buller, who was involved in various conflicts, including the Zulu War of 1879. He later served in two Boer Wars. There have been numerous landlords and landladies since then. This aerial view over the town centre below dates from 1931. Looking rather more built up here, as Bude begins to develop as a popular tourist destination.

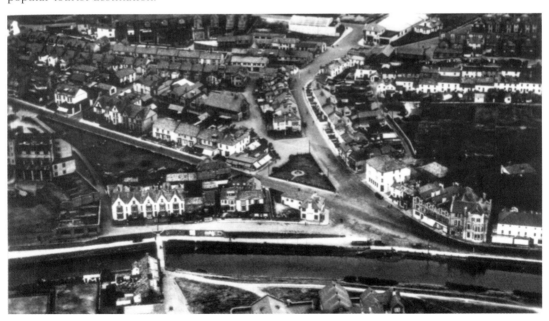

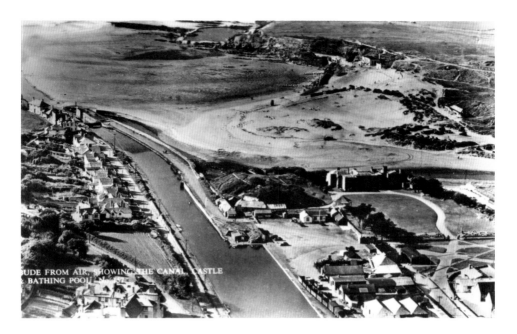

Aerial View of Bude

This is an aerial shot from the 1950s, showing the canal, castle and Bude Sea Pool. Summerleaze Beach, with the Downs, is clearly visible, as are the houses along Breakwater Road to the left of the canal, but we can see that Bude is still pretty underdeveloped at this time. Old Bude from the town is the subject of the second card below. Bude was growing in the nineteenth century but depended upon Stratton for many things. Rennie Bere and Bryan Dudley Stamp, in their book on the area, quote Canon Maskell, from 1872, who wrote of a sailor enquiring about a doctor in Bude. The reply was '... when the quality's here in the summer us sends across to Stratton but in winter us just dies a natural death', which implies that tourism was the lifeblood of the town, and describes its seasonal nature even then.

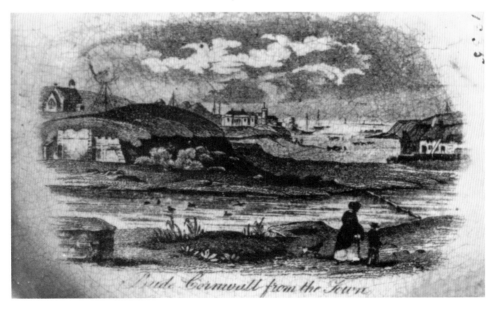

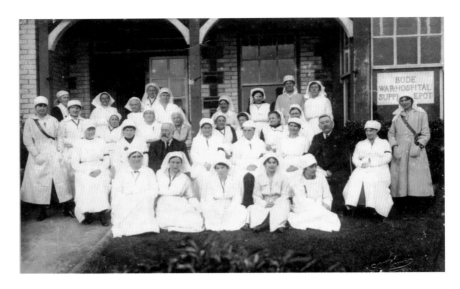

Bude War Hospital, c. 1915/16, and Coronation Day, 1911

This is Bude War Hospital Supply Depot c. 1915/16, set up and run by a Mrs Gray, who lived at a property called Orlebar. It did not care for patients, but like others dotted up and down the UK, manufactured surgical dressings, bandages and so on. Every month, these were shipped to central depots where they were catalogued, sorted and packaged for onwards dispatch to hospitals receiving the sick and wounded in the UK and France. The ladies and men you see would all be local volunteers, with the raw materials for goods they manufactured provided by subscriptions they paid and collections made in the Bude area. Thanks to Tim Moreman, a local, for this information. Coronation Day, 1911, also features here below. 22 June was the Coronation Day of George V. He reigned until his death in 1936. The Coronation itself took place at Westminster Abbey, but there were celebrations everywhere for this major royal occasion, including Bude. It was definitely a day to put the flags out. This postcard shows the church parade near the Falcon Swing Bridge.

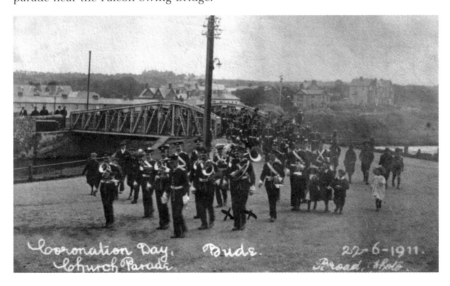

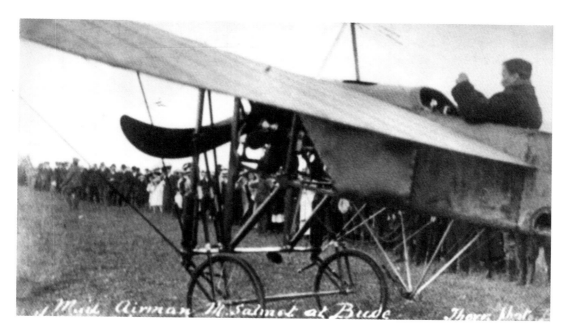

Aviation Tour and Empire Day

The *Daily Mail*, it seems, sponsored an aeroplane tour as an advertisement. It sent a plane around the country in 1912 to show off the wonders of aviation. It was a Bleriot 80 HP Monoplane, piloted by early aviator Monsieur Salmet. Here he is at Bude, probably in the area known as Broadclose. Salmet flew the Bleriot XI from Bude to Lawhitton near Launceston, then onto Newquay, but was unfortunately forced down for repairs at Bodmin. Bude likes celebrating. Below is a celebration of Empire Day in 1906. The Duke of Cornwall's Light Infantry pose in front of the Drill Hall. Today, it is Neetside Community Centre, but also one of Bude's early Methodist chapels.

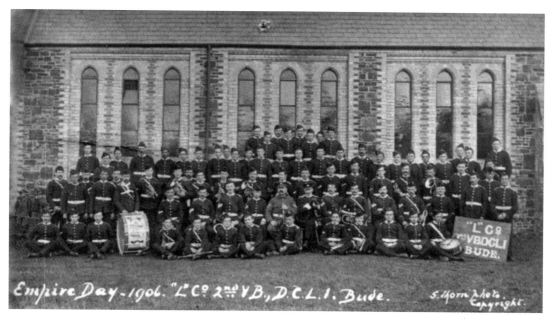

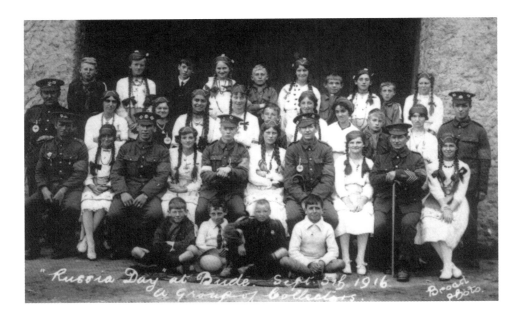

"Russia Day" at Bude. Sept 5th 1916. A Group of Collectors.

Russia Day and the Golf Club Committee

Russia Day is a strange one. It was something which seems to have taken place at various locations during the First World War, in order to exhibit solidarity and collect clothes and other items for the Russian troops. The above view shows those involved in 1916. Not quite sure what Bude's Russian link was, though Tolstoy is once said to have visited the town. Golf is rather more explicable. The Golf Club Committee, 1906, is shown on this card below, on the occasion of a professional golf tournament featuring British and US Open winner Harry Vardon, who hailed from Jersey. North Cornwall Golf Club was formed in 1891, playing on Summerleaze Down. Bude Golf Club was later formed, becoming Bedes Haven, and eventually Bude and North Cornwall Golf Club. Bude Golf course area was possibly previously called Sandy Common during the Battle of Stamford Hill, 1643.

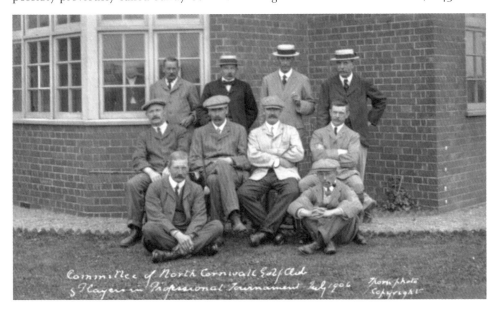

Committee of North Cornwall Golf Club & Players in Professional Tournament July 1906

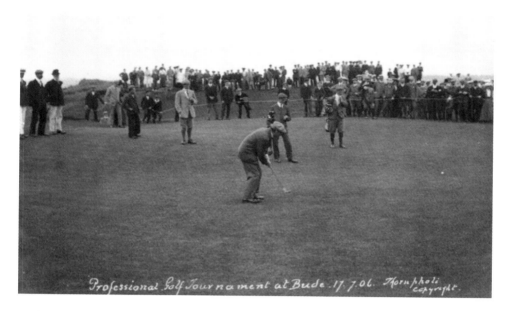

Professional Golf Tournament at Bude. 17.7.06. Hornphoto copyright.

Bude Attractions

With an action shot of a professional golf tournament at Bude, this card promotes one of Bude's many attractions. The land between the town and coast is quite tight and breezy, but it has not prevented high standards of golf at this seaside golf course, which remains popular with locals and visitors. Oddly, the opening of new sewage works in 1909 was also an event (*below*). Hard to believe that such a crowd would gather for something like this, but sewerage treatment was an issue then and any opportunity for a celebration was not to be missed. Here, a crowd gathers on Efford Down in 1909 to mark the opening of the town's new sewage works, which discharged the effluent through a valve at the base of the cliff at each high tide.

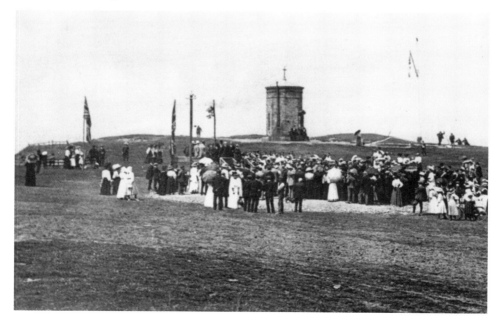

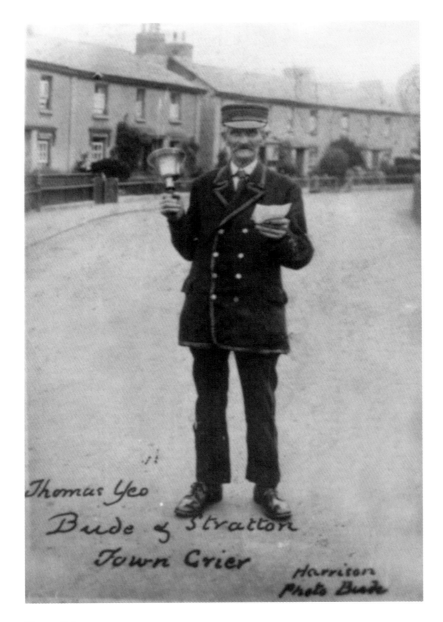

Thomas Yeo
Bude & Stratton
Town Crier

Harrison
Photo Bude

Town Crier

Thomas Yeo was Bude's town crier in 1912. It's rather odd that Bude had a town crier because they were generally employed by the courts to proclaim information as required. To my knowledge, Bude did not have a court, though neighbouring Stratton did. Maybe he was just there to give public notices.

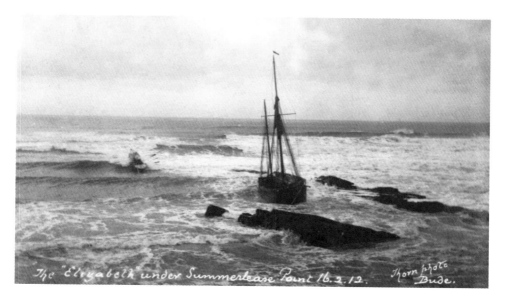

The "Elizabeth" under Summerlease Point 16.2.12.   Thorn photo Bude.

Bude Ships

The shore around Bude was treacherous for old sailing ships. The *Elizabeth*, among the rocks at Sharpnose Point, is shown here in 1913. The *Georgina* had been wrecked here in 1865. The North Cornwall coast is a lee shore, which means that boats drift if sails or an engine break. Hence, many boats were mercilessly blown onto rocks by prevailing south westerly winds. The second view of *Elizabeth* shows the crew on the boat at Summerleaze in 1912. In 1913, there is a record of the Bude Lifeboat being launched to a ketch called *Elizabeth*, saving five, but no other details are available. The harbour was hazardous due to awkward tides and rough seas, so ships were often met by 'hobblers' outside the harbour, who were basically sailors in rowing boats piloting and roping in the ships to safe course.

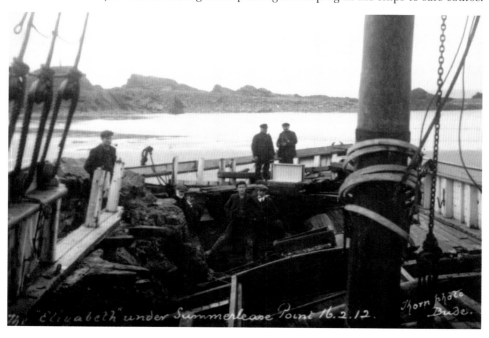

The "Elizabeth" under Summerleaze Point 16.2.12.   Thorn photo Bude.

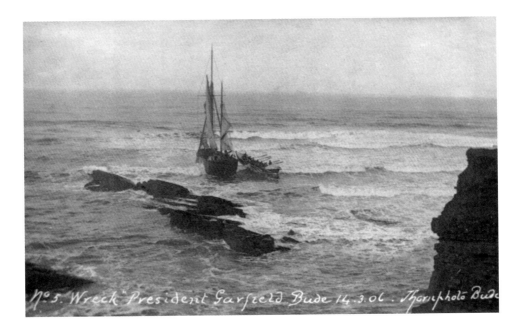

No 5. Wreck "President Garfield" Bude 14.3.06 : Thorn photo Bude

Lifeboats

President Garfield 1906. Lots of ships were named after President Garfield. According to Bude Lifeboat website, this ketch was built in 1881 at Amlwch, originally as a schooner. She was converted to a ketch rig before being sold to John Banbury of Bude in 1897. Bude's Frederick Martin became her master. In 1906, she was stranded on Coach Rock, just off Summerleaze, requiring launch of the Bude Lifeboat to rescue the crew of three, which included a boy. The Bude Lifeboat website mentions that in 1903, a profit from Lifeboat Day of £38 was handed over to the treasurer. A lifeboat was apparently stationed at Bude for a short time in 1817, but was allowed to fall into disrepair. By 1852, the rocket apparatus had arrived. The *Royal William* boat was given in 1837, but was unstable and capsized, drowning two crew on exercises in the harbour. In 1853, she was replaced, and ten years later the lifeboat house (now a holiday cottage) near the Falcon was built.

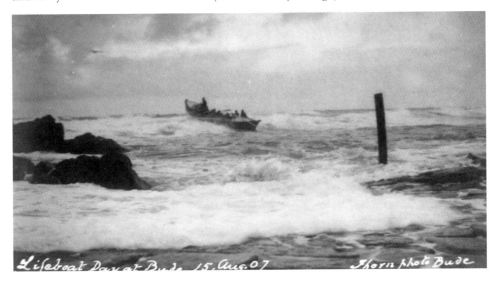

Lifeboat Day at Bude. 15. Aug. 07   Thorn photo Bude

Bude Lifeboat

In February, 1904, the *Wild Pigeon*, captained by John Hallett, was swept away from her mooring in the canal when the inner lock gate was broken by a huge wave, becoming stranded at Summerleaze, wrecked under the cliffs there. She had been wrecked once before in 1989 with her crew rescued by rocket apparatus and breeches buoy. The Bude lifeboat was launched on 11 May 1909, to the steam trawler *Scotia*, stranded in dense fog just above Northcott Mouth, according to the Bude Lifeboat website. There's quite a crowd here. The sea was smooth and the captain and crew hoped to refloat her on the high tide so refused to leave the vessel, despite her dangerous position among rocks and pounding sea. Despite all precautions, it seems the *Scotia* required no further aid, so she was one of the lucky ones.

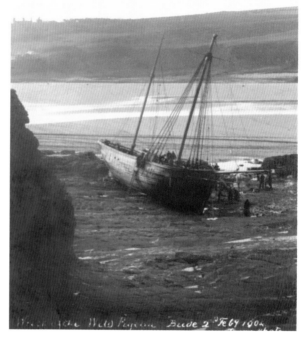

Wreck of the Wild Pigeon. Bude 2nd Feby 1904

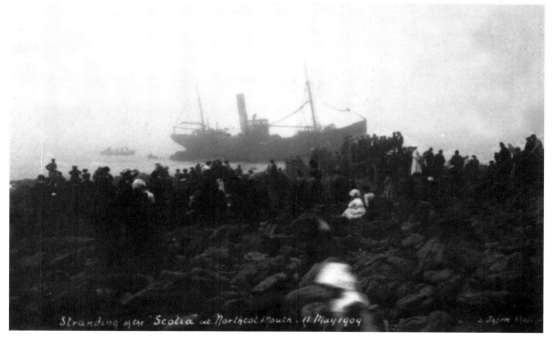

Stranding of the Scotia at Northcott Mouth. 11 May 1909

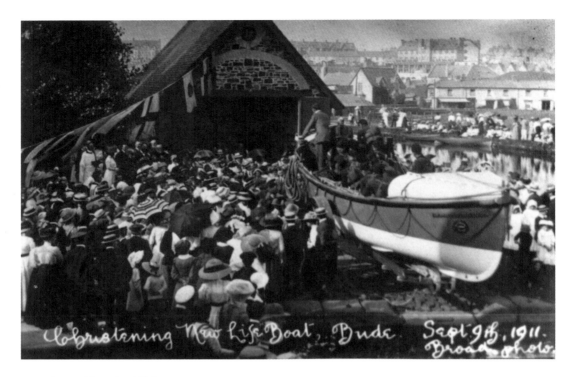

Launching the Lifeboat

Launching the lifeboat was never an easy task in Bude. There were two options – taking the boat down the canal and through the lock gates, which was time-consuming and only worked if tide and conditions allowed. The other way was to launch it via a carriage drawn by ten cart horses galloping into the waves. The first practice of the new lifeboat is shown here, in 1911. This was the self-righting Elizabeth Moore Garden. After 1852, the lifeboat was backed by rocket apparatus, kept in the rocket house at the end of Breakwater Road, manned by the coastguards. This device was invented by an engineering Cornishman, Trengrouse of Helston.

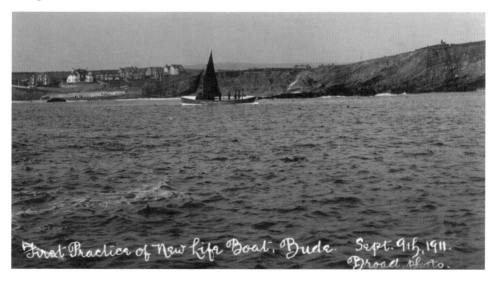

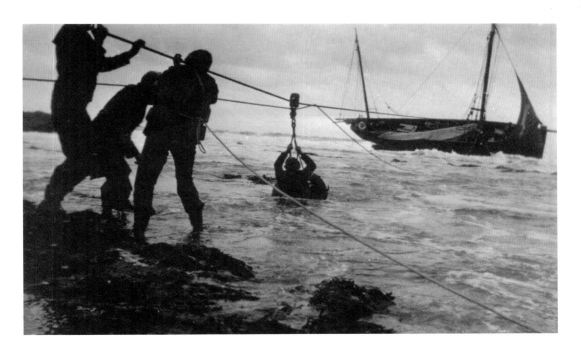

Jeannot

This dramatic picture shows the rescue of the crew of the French sloop *Jeannot*, which was driven ashore in a gale at Millook on 24 June 1919. The crew members were taken off by breeches buoy, sent over from the shore by the rocket apparatus. Launching the lifeboat remained a tough task in Bude, which now has an inshore inflatable boat to cope with the rocky inlets. A wonderful image here of the horses galloping out to sea to launch the lifeboat. I'm not sure if the horses went willingly into the choppy waters but it seemed to work. It wasn't until 1921 that the caterpillar tractor arrived in Bude for (then unsuccessful) trials at pulling the lifeboat.

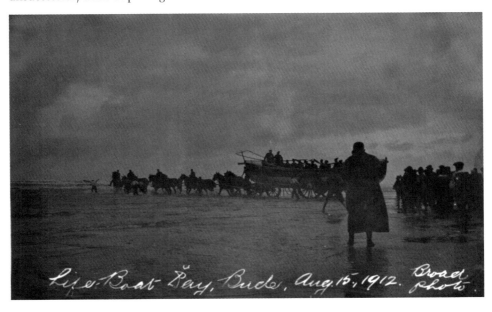

Life-Boat Bay, Bude, Aug. 15, 1912. Broad photo.

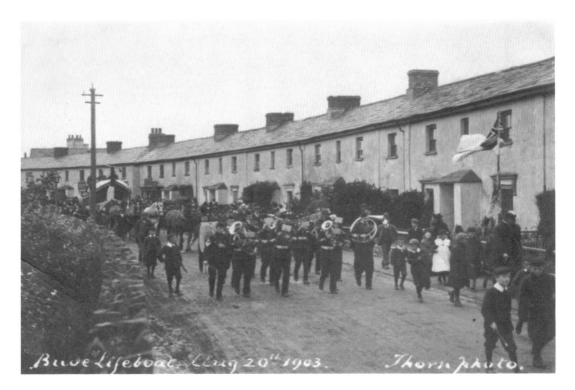

Bude Lifeboat Aug 20th 1903.   Thorn photo.

Lifeboat Day

Even today the town band and other processions take place in Bude, but usually on Carnival Day rather than Lifeboat Day. This lifeboat procession in 1903 is around the Crescent, the road by the Tourist Information Centre from the canal area to the Strand. After 1923, Bude had no lifeboat but developed an inshore rescue station, established near the lock gates.

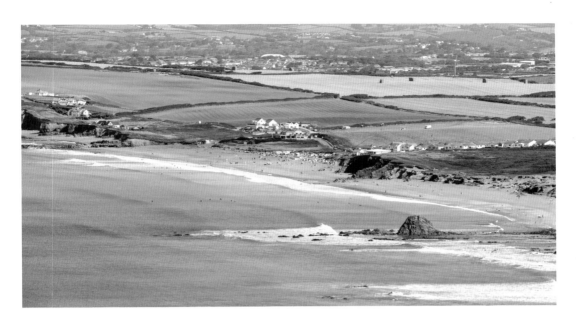

The Breakwater

Back in 1937, a journalist is reputed to have said that Bude had no rival. Local people and many visitors still agree. Thankfully, the tourist guides are now more tasteful than in the past. Even as late as 1973, the cover of the Bude tourist guide was decorated with a bikini-clad girl (daughter, it is alleged, of the then town clerk), which, along with the wording, caused some controversy. There were also claims to having little rainfall, but meteorology seems to bear it out that Bude does enjoy something of a micro-climate with, on the whole, good weather. If the weather is poor, the Breakwater is not the place to be. The first Breakwater was destroyed in 1838. It was steep sided and had a pier head. The new one was less pretentious, only 4 feet above high water at spring tide, so the angle was lower and resistance to waves minimal, according to Bere and Dudley Stamp. This made it a more effective and lasting structure.

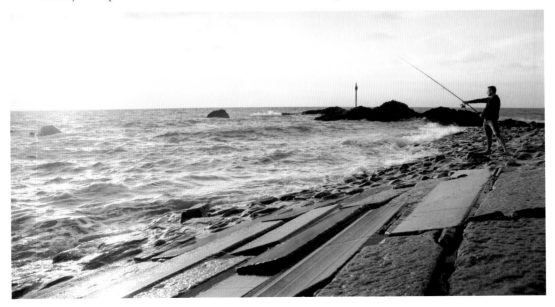

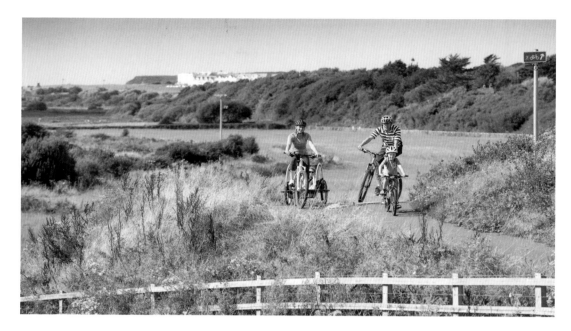

Bude Canal, Marshes and Dunes

Bude Canal and Marshes has a Green Flag award for its abundance of wildlife such as otters and kingfishers. A walk along the canal is a delight, with an abundance of flora and fauna. One of my favourite occupations is taking a book to the dunes on a sunny day, pausing occasionally to watch the waves (and the surfing). Dunes are caused when the wind blows up the beach (strong onshore winds are useful for this saltation) until the sands hit an obstacle. Sand builds up over time, specialist plants such as culm grow, and the dunes develop. This is a very simplistic explanation, but the dunes are a great place to find a sun trap.

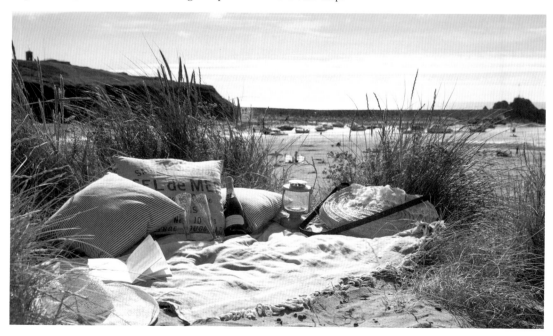

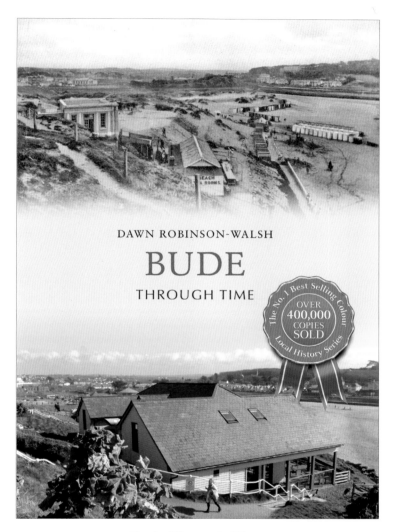

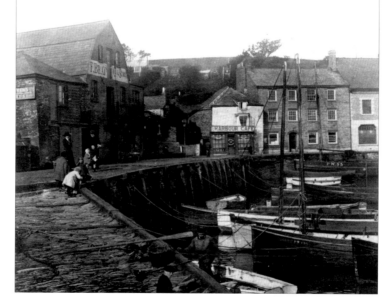

MALCOLM McCARTHY

PADSTOW
HISTORY TOUR

Padstow History Tour

Malcolm McCarthy

Join author Malcolm McCarthy as he takes the reader on a tour of
the seaside town of Padstow, charting the historic sites and streets
along the way

978 1 4456 4631 2

96 pages, full colour

n all good bookshops or order direct
website www.amberley-books.com